THE

ROLL OF BATTLE ABBEY.

CLAYTON & CO., PRINTERS,
16 HART STREET, COVENT GARDEN.

THE ROLL OF BATTLE ABBEY,

Annotated.

BY

JOHN BERNARD BURKE, ESQ.,

AUTHOR OF

"THE PEERAGE," "LANDED GENTRY," &c.

> "This folk of Normandie
> Among us woneth yet, and shalleth evermoe."
> *Robert of Gloucester.*

London:
EDWARD CHURTON, 26, HOLLES STREET.
MDCCCXLVIII.

Notice

In many older books, foxing (or discoloration) occurs and, in some instances, print lightens with wear and age. Reprinted books, such as this, often duplicate these flaws, notwithstanding efforts to reduce or eliminate them. The pages of this reprint have been digitally enhanced and, where possible, the flaws eliminated in order to provide clarity of content and a pleasant reading experience.

by John Bernard Burke, Esq., 1848

Originally published
London:
1848

Reprinted by:
Janaway Publishing, Inc.
2015

Janaway Publishing
732 Kelsey Ct.
Santa Maria, California 93454
(805) 925-1038
www.janawaygenealogy.com

ISBN: 978-1-59641-349-8

Made in the United States of America

TO

WILLIAM EDWARD SURTEES, Esq., D.C.L.,

THE AUTHOR'S KIND AND EVER-VALUED FRIEND,

THIS LITTLE VOLUME

Is inscribed,

WITH FEELINGS OF THE SINCEREST REGARD AND ESTEEM.

Brompton, July 10, 1848.

CONTENTS.

THE ROLL OF BATTLE ABBEY, according to Hollinshed	.	.	2
,, ,, according to Brompton	.	.	8
,, ,, according to Duchesne	.	.	8*
,, ,, according to Leland	.	.	11*
ANNOTATIONS, descriptive of the various families descended from the Normans	. . . . .	.	11
INDEX			

THE
ROLL OF BATTLE ABBEY.

Danaûm proceres, Agamemnoniæque phalanges.

The Roll of Battle Abbey, the earliest record of the Normans, has at all times been regarded with deep interest, by the principal families of the kingdom—by those who shew descent directly from the chiefs of the Conqueror's host, as well as by those who indirectly establish a similar lineage.

The Abbey of Battle, a memorial of one of the most important events in English history, was erected upon a plain called Heathfield, about seven miles distant from Hastings, in fulfilment of a vow made by the Conqueror prior to the battle which won for him the diadem of England. Within a year, the foundation was laid on the very spot where the battle of Hastings had been fought, and but a brief period subsequently passed, until the Monastery itself arose in all its magnificence, richly endowed and highly privileged, dedicated to the honour of the Holy Trinity and St. Martin, the high altar standing where Harold and the Saxon standard fell. The Conqueror at first designed that this great religious House should accommodate one hundred and forty monks, but provision appears to have been made for sixty only. The first community, a society of Benedictines, came from Marmonstier, in Normandy, and were enjoined to pray for those who died in the battle, and to preserve a faithful record of all who shared in the glory of the victory. Thus arose the Abbey of Battle, and thus the Roll of Battle Abbey.

The endowments of the royal founder upon the Abbey and the holy Brethren, were in the extreme liberal and munificent. Aldsiston in Sussex, Lymsfield in Surrey, How in Essex, Craumere in Oxon, and Briswalderton in Berks, together with a league of land around the house itself, were but a portion of their vast domains. They had beside the churches of Radings and Colunton, in Devon, and St. Olave, in Exeter. The immunities they enjoyed were alike considerable. Their grand charter exempted the brethren of Battle from episcopal jurisdiction, treasure-trove, and free warren. The Abbot wore the Mitre, and was invested with a power to pardon any felon whom he might chance to meet with going to execution. From foundation to dissolution the Abbey of Battle had a succession of thirty-one mitred Abbots; the last, John Hammond, was chosen in 1529. The site of the dissolved abbey was granted by Henry VIII. to Richard Gilmer, who sold the estate to Sir Anthony Browne, from whose descendants, the Brownes, Viscounts Montague, the abbey and lands passed again by sale to Sir Thomas Webster, Bart., in whose family they are yet vested. The still extant ruins, computed at not less than a mile of ground, bear ample testimony to the splendour and magnificence of the celebrated Monastery of Battle.

The Table containing the following names was formerly suspended in the Abbey, with this inscription:—

> Dicitur a bello, bellum locus hic, quia bello
> Angligenæ victi, sunt hic in morte relicti:
> Martyris in Christi festo cecidere Calixti:
> Sexagenus erat sextus millessimus annus
> Cum pereunt Angli, stella monstrante cometâ.

Aumarle	Arcy and Akeny	Bounilaine
Aincourt	Albeny	Bois
Audeley	Aybeuare	Botelere
Angillam	Amay	Bourcher
Argentoune	Aspermound	Brabaion
Arundel	Amerenges	Berners
Auenant		Braibuf
Abell	Bertram	Brand and Brouce
Arwerne	Buttecourt	Burgh
Aunwers	Brebus and Bysey	Bushy
Angers	Bardolfe	Banet
Angenoun	Basset and Bigot	Blondell
Archere	Bohun	Breton
Anuay	Bailif	Bluat and Baious
Asperuile	Bondeville	Browne
Abbevile	Brabason	Beke
Andevile	Baskervile	Bikard
Amouedruile	Bures	Banastre

Baloun
Beauchampe
Bray and Bandy
Bracy
Boundes
Bascoun
Broilem
Broleuy
Burnell
Bellet
Baudewin
Beaumont
Burdon
Berteuilay
Barre
Busseuille
Blunt
Baupere
Bevill
Barduedor
Brette
Barrett
Bonrett
Bainard
Barnivale
Bonett
Bary
Bryan
Bodin
Beteuruille
Bertin
Bereneuille
Bellew
Beuery
Bushell
Boranuile
Browe
Beleuers
Buffard
Bonueier
Boteville

Bellire
Bastard
Brasard
Beelhelme
Braine
Brent
Braunch
Belesur
Blundell
Burdett
Bagott
Beauuise
Belemis
Beisin
Bernon
Boels
Belefroun
Brutz
Barchampe

Camois
Camvile
Chawent
Cauncy
Conderay
Colvile
Chamberlaine
Chambernoun
Comin
Columber
Cribett
Creuquere
Corbine
Corbett
Chaundos
Chaworth
Cleremaus
Clarell
Chopis
Chaunduit
Chantelow

Chamberay
Cressy
Curtenay
Conestable
Cholmeley
Champney
Chawnos
Coinivile
Champaine
Careuile
Carbonelle
Charles
Chereberge
Chawnes
Chaumont
Caperoun
Cheine
Curson
Couille
Chaiters
Cheines
Cateray
Cherecourt
Cammile
Clerenay
Curly
Cuily
Clinels
Clifford.

Denaville
Derey
Dive, or Dyne
Dispencere
Daubeney
Daniel
Deuise and Druell
Devaus
Davers
Dodingsels
Darell

B 2

Delaber
De la Pole
Delalinde
Delahill
Delaware
Delauache
Dakeny
Dauntre
Desny
Dabernoune
Damry
Daueros
Dauonge
Duilby
Delauere
Delahoid
Durange
Delee
Delaund
Delaward
Delaplanch
Damnot
Danway
Deheuse
Deuile
Disard
Doiville
Durand
Drury
Dabitott
Dunsterville
Dunchamp
Dambelton

Estrange
Estuteville
Engaine
Estriels
Esturney

Ferrerers

Folvile
Fitz-Water
Fitz-Marmaduke
Fleuez
Filberd
Fitz-Roger
Fauecourt
Ferrers
Fitz-Philip
Foliot
Furnieueus
Fitz-Otes
Fitz-William
Fitz-Roand
Fitz-Pain
Fitz-Auger
Fitz-Aleyn
Fitz-Rauf
Fitz-Browne
Fouke
Frevile
Front de Boef
Facunburge
Forz
Frisell
Fitz-Simon
Fitz-Fouk
Folioll
Fitz-Thomas
Fitz-Morice
Fitz-Hugh
Fitz-Henrie
Fitz-Waren
Fitz-Rainold
Flamvile
Formay
Fitz-Eustach
Fitz-Lawrence
Formibaud
Frisound
Finere

Fitz-Robert
Furnivall
Fitz-Geffrey
Fitz-Herbert
Fitz-Peres
Fitchet
Fitz-Rowes
Fitz-Fitz
Fitz-John
Fleschampe

Gurnay
Gressy
Graunson
Gracy
Georges
Gower
Gaugy
Goband
Gray
Gaunson
Golofre
Gobion
Grensy
Graunt
Greile
Grenet
Gurry
Gurley
Grammori
Gernoun
Grendoun
Gurdon
Guines
Griuel
Grenuile
Glateuile
Giffard
Gouerges
Gamages.

Hauteny
Haunsard
Hastings
Hanlay
Haurell
Husee
Hercy
Herion
Herne
Harecourt
Henoure
Houell
Hamelin
Harewell
Hardell
Haket
Hamound
Harcord

Jarden
Jay
Jeniels
Jerconuise
Januile
Jasperuile

Kaunt
Karre
Karrowe
Keine
Kimaronne
Kiriell
Kancey
Kenelre

Loueney
Lacy
Linnebey
Latomer
Loveday
Lovell
Lemare
Leuetot
Lucy
Luny
Logeuile
Longespes
Louerace
Longechampe
Lascales
Louan
Leded
Luse
Loterell
Loruge
Longueuale
Loy
Lorancourt
Loious
Limers
Longepay
Laumale
Lane
Lovetot

Mohant
Mowne
Maundeville
Marmilon
Moribray
Morvile
Miriel
Maulay
Malebrauch
Malemaine
Mortimere
Mortimaine
Muse
Marteine
Mountbother
Mountsoler
Maleuile

Malet
Mounteney
Monfichet
Maleherbe
Mare
Musegros
Musarde
Moine
Montrauers
Merke
Murres
Mortiualu
Monchenesy
Mallony
Marny
Mountagu
Mountford
Maule
Monthernon
Musett
Menevile
Manteuenant
Manse
Menpincoy
Maine
Mainard
Morell
Mainell
Maleluse
Memorous
Morreis
Morleian Maine
Malevere
Mandut
Mountmarten
Mantolet
Miners
Mauclerke
Maunchenell
Mouett
Meintenore

THE ROLL OF BATTLE ABBEY.

Meletak
Manuile
Mangisere
Maumasin
Mountlouel
Maurewarde
Monhaut
Meller
Mountgomerie
Manlay
Maularde
Menere
Martinaste
Mainwaring
Matelay
Malemis
Maleheire
Moren
Melun
Marceaus
Maiell
Morton

Noell
Nevile
Newmarch
Norbet
Norice
Newborough
Neirement
Neile
Normavile
Neofmarche
Nermitz
Nembrutz

Otevell
Olibef
Olifant
Olenel
Olsell
Olifard

Ounell
Orioll

Pigot
Pery
Perepound
Pershale
Power
Painell
Peche and Pauey
Pevrell
Perot
Picard
Pinkenie
Pomeray
Pounce
Paveley
Paifrere
Plunkenet
Phuars
Punchardoun
Pinchard
Placy
Pugoy
Patefine
Place
Pampilivum
Percelay
Perere and Pekeny
Poterell
Peukeney
Peccell
Pinell
Putrill
Petiuoll
Preaus
Pantolf
Peito
Penecord
Preuerlirlegast
Percivale

Quinci
Quintini

Ros
Ridell
Rivers
Riuell
Rous
Rushell
Raband
Ronde
Rie
Rokell
Risers
Randiule
Roselin
Rastoke
Rinuill
Rougere
Rait
Ripere
Rigny
Richmound
Rochford
Raimond

Souch
Seeuile
Shucheus
Senclere
Sent Quintin
Sent Omere
Sent Amond
Sent Legere
Somervile
Sieward
Saunsourre
Sanford
Sanctos
Sauay
Saulay

Sule
Sorell
Somerey
Sent John
Sent George
Sent Les
Seffe
Saluin
Say
Solers
Sent Albin
Sent Martin
Sourdemale
Seguin
Sent Barbe
Sent Vile
Suremounte
Soreglise
Sandvile
Sauncey
Sirewast
Sent Cheveroll
Sent More
Sent Scudemore

Toget
Tercy
Tuchet
Tracy
Trousbut
Trainell
Taket
Trussell
Trison
Talbot
Tonny
Traies
Tollemach
Tolous
Tanny
Touke
Tibtote
Turbevile
Turvile
Tomy and Tavernez
Trenchevile
Trenchilion
Tankervile
Tirell
Trivet
Tolet
Travers
Tardevile
Tinevile
Torell
Tortechapell
Treverell
Tenwis
Totelles

Vere
Vernoun
Vesey
Verdoune
Valence
Verdeire
Vavasour
Vendore
Verlay
Valenger
Venables
Venoure
Vilan
Verland
Valers
Veirney
Vauurile
Veniels
Verrere
Vschere
Vessay
Vanay
Vian
Vernoys
Vrnall
Vnket
Vrnaful
Vasderoll
Vaberon
Valingford
Venecorde
Valiue
Viuille
Vancorde and
Valenges

Wardebois
Ward
Wafre
Wake
Wareine
Wate
Watelin
Watevil
Wely
Werdonell
Wespaile
Wivell

In completion of our design of indicating the names of the Norman Chieftains who accompanied the Conqueror—we annex another catalogue, extracted from *Brompton's Chronicle*:—

Liste des Conquerants d'Angleterre.

"Mandevile et Dandevile, Omfravile et Domfrevile, Botevile et Baskervile, Evile et Clevile, Warbevile et Carvile, Botevile et Stotevile, Morevile et Colevile, Deverous et Canvile, Mohun et Bohun, Vipont et Vinon, Baylon et Bayloun, Maris et Marmion, Agulis et Agulon, Chamberlain et Chamberson, Ver et Vernon, Verdeis et Verdum, Criel et Cardon, Danver et Davernon, Hasting et Camois, Bardolph Botes et Boys, Garenne et Gardeboys, Rodes et Deverois, Auris et Argenton, Botelour et Boutevilain, Malebouche et Malemain, Hautevile et Hautain, Dauney et Deveyne, Malin et Malvoisin, Morton et Mortemer, Brause et Colombier, Saint Denis et Saint Cler, Saint Aubin et Saint Omer, Saint Philbert Fyens et Gomer, Turbevile et Turbemer, Georges et Spenser, Brus et Botteler, Crenawell et Saint Quintin, Devereux et Saint Martin, Saint Mor et Saint Leger, Saint Vigor et Saint Per, Avenel et Paynel, Payver et Perdel, Riviers et Rivell, Beauchamp et Beaupel, Lon et Lovell, Rose et Druel, Montabons et Monsorel, Trussebot et Trassel, Burgas et Burnell, Bray et Botterell, Biset et Basset, Malevile et Mallet, Bonevil et Bonet, Nervil et Narbet, Coinel et Corbet, Montain et Mont Fichet, Genevile et Giffard, Say et Sewrard, Cari et Chaward, Harecourt et Hansard, Musgrave et Musard, Mare et Mantravers, Ferry et Ferrers, Barnevil et Berniers, Cheyne et Chaliers, Danudon et Dangiers, Versey, Gray et Grangers, Bertran et Bigot, Trayley et Traygod, Penbert et Pigot, Freyn et Foliot, Dapison et Talbôt, Sauraver et Sanford, Vagu et Veutort, Montagu et Mouford, Forneus et Fornevous, Valens, Yle et Vaus, Clarel et Clarus, Aubevel et Saint Amous, Agos et Dragous, Malherbe et Maudut, Breves et Chaudut, Fitz Oures et Fitz de Lou, Contenor et Cantelon, Braibeuf et Hulbins, Bolebek et Molyns, Moleton et Besil, Rochford et Dosevil, Wartevil et Davil, Nevers et Nevil, Heynous, Burs, Burdevon, Ylebon, Hyldebrond et Helion, Loges et Saint Lore, Moubank et Saint Malo, Wake et Wakevil, Caudray et Knevil, Scalier et Cleremont, Beaumis et Beaumont, Mons et Monchamp, Noters et Nowchamp, Percy, Cruce et Lacy, Quincy et Tracy, Greyley et Saint Velery, Pinkeni et Pavely, Monhaut et Monchessy, Lovein et Lucy, Artos et Arcy, Grevil et Courcy, Arras et Cressy, Merle et Moubray, Gornay et Courtnay, Hauslaing et Turnay, Husée et Husay, Ponchardin et Pomeray, Longevil et Longue Espée, Payns et Pontelarge, Strange et Sauvage."

Duchesne gives this ancient List of the Conquerors of England, as derived from a Charter in Battle Abbey. It is very similar to, but is not so full as, that published by Hollingshed.

Aumerle
Audeley
Angilliam
Argentoun
Arundell
Avenant
Abel
Awgers
Angenoun
Archer
Aspervile.
Amonerdvile
Arey
Akeny
Albeny
Asperemound

Bertram
Buttecourt
Brœchus
Byseg
Bardolf
Basset
Bohun
Baylife
Bondeville
Barbason
Beer
Bures
Bonylayne
Barbayon
Berners
Braybuf
Brand
Bonvile
Burgh

Busshy
Blundell
Breton
Belasyse
Bowser
Bayons
Bulmere
Brone
Beke
Bowlers
Banestre
Belomy
Belknape
Beauchamp
Bandy
Broyleby
Burnel
Belot
Beufort
Baudewine
Burdon
Berteviley
Barte
Bussevile
Blunt
Beawper
Bret
Barret
Barnevale
Barry
Bodyt
Bertevile
Bertine
Belew
Buschell
Beleners

Buffard
Boteler
Botvile
Brasard
Belbelme
Braunche
Bolesur
Blundel
Burdet
Bigot
Beaupount
Bools
Belefroun
Barchampe

Camos
Chanville
Chawent
Chancy
Couderay
Colvile
Chamberlaine
Chambernoune
Cribet
Corbine
Corbet
Coniers
Chaundos
Coucy
Chaworthe
Claremaus
Clarell
Camnine
Chaunduyt
Clarways
Chantilowe

B 3

Colet
Cressy
Courtenay
Constable
Chancer
Cholmelay
Corlevile
Champeney
Carew
Chawnos
Clarvaile
Champaine
Carbonell
Charles
Chareberge
Chawnes
Chawmont
Cheyne
Cursen
Conell
Chayters
Cheynes
Cateray
Cherecourt
Chaunvile
Clereney
Curly
Clyfford

Deauvile
Dercy
Dine
Dispencer
Daniel
Denyse
Druell
Devaus
Davers
Doningsels
Darell

Delabere
De la Pole
De la Lind
De la Hill
De la Wate
De la Watche
Dakeny
Dauntre
Desuye
Dabernoune
Damry
Daveros
De la Vere
De Liele
De la Warde
De la Planch
Danway
De Hewse
Disard
Durant
Divy

Estrange
Estutaville
Escriols
Engayne
Evers
Esturney

Folvile
Fitz Water
Fitz Marmaduk
Fibert
Fitz Roger
Fitz Robert
Fanecourt
Fitz Philip
Fitz William
Fitz Paine
Fitz Alyne

Fitz Raulfe
Fitz Browne
Foke
Frevile
Faconbrige
Frissel
Filioll
Fitz Thomas
Fitz Morice
Fitz Hughe
Fitz Warren
Faunvile
Formay
Formiband
Frison
Finer
Fitz Urcy
Furnivall
Fitz Herbert
Fitz John

Gargrave
Graunson
Gracy
Glaunvile
Gover
Gascoyne
Gray
Golofer
Grauns
Gurly
Gurdon
Gamages
Gaunt

Hansard
Hastings
Haulay
Husie
Herne

Hamelyn
Harewell
Hardel
Hecket
Hamound
Harecord

Jarden
Jay
Janvile
Jasparvile

Karre
Karron
Kyriell

Lestrange
Levony
Latomere
Loveday
Logenton
Level
Lescrope
Lemare
Litterile
Lucy
Lisley or Liele
Longspes
Lonschampe
Lastels
Lindsey
Loterel
Longvaile
Lewawse
Loy
Lave
Le Despenser

Marmilon
Moribray

Morvil
Manley
Malebranche
Malemaine
Muschampe
Musgrave
Mesni-le-Villers
Mortmaine
Muse
Marteine
Mountbocher
Malevile
Mountney
Maleherbe
Musgros
Musard
Mautravers
Merke
Murres
Montagu
Montalent
Mandute
Manle
Malory
Merny
Muffet
Menpincoy
Mainard
Morell
Morley
Mountmartin Yners
Mauley
Mainwaring
Mantell
Mayel
Morton

Nevile
Neumarche
Norton

Norbet
Norece
Newborough
Neele
Normanvile

Otenel
Olibef
Olifaunt
Oysell
Oliford
Oryoll

Pigot
Pecy
Perecount
Pershale
Power
Paynel
Peche
Peverell
Perot
Picard
Pudsey
Pimeray
Pounsey
Punchardon
Pynchard
Placy
Patine
Pampilion
Poterell
Pekeney
Pervinke
Penicord

Quincy
Quintine

Rose

Ridle	Seint-Scudemor	Vavasour
Rynel		Vender
Rous	Tows	Verder
Russel	Toget	Verdon
Rond	Talybois	Aubrie de Vere
Richmond	Tuchet	Vernoune
Rocheford	Truslot	Verland
Reymond	Trusbut	Verlay
	Traynel	Vernois
Seuche	Taket	Verny
Seint-Quintine	Talbot	Vilan
Seint-Omer	Tanny	
Seint-Amand	Tibtote	Unframvile
Seint-Léger	Trussell	Unket
Sovervile	Turbevile	Urnall
Sanford	Turvile	
Somery	Torel	Wake
Seint-George	Tavers	Waledger
Seint-Lés	Torel	War.'e
Savine	Tirell	Wardebus
Seint-Clo	Totels	Waren
Seint-Albine	Taverner	Wate
Seinte-Barbe		Wateline
Sandevile	Valence	Watevile
Seint-More	Vancord	Woly
		Wywell

Leland* has two lists:—

I.

Un role de ceux queux veignont in Angleterre ovesque roy William la Conquereur.

Faet asavoir que en l'an du grace nostre seigneur Jesu Christe mil sisaunt ses, per jour de samadi en la feste S. Calixte, vint William Bastarde duc del Normandie, cosin à noble roy seint Edwarde le fiz de Emme de Angleter, et tua le roy Haraude, et lui tali le terre par l'eide des Normannez et aultres gents de divers terres. Entre quils vint ovesque lui monseir William de Moion le Veil, le plus noble de tout l'oste. Cist William de Moion avoit de sa retenaunde en l'ost tous les grauntz sieignors après nomez, si come il

---

* Collectanea de rebus Britannicis, ed. Hearne, i. 202.

est escript en le liver des conquerors, s'est à savoir : Raol Taisson de Cinqueleis ; Roger Marmion le Veil ; Monsieur Nel de Sein Saviour ; Raol de Gail qui fust Briton ; Avenel de Giars ; Hubert Paignel ; Robert Berthram ; Raol le archer de Val et le seir de Bricoil ; li sires de Sole et le sires de Sureval ; li sires de S. Jehan, et li sires de Breal ; li sires de Breus et due sens des homez ; li sires de S. Seu et li sires de Cuallie ; li sires de Cenullie, et li sire de Basqueville ; li sires de Praels, et li sires de Souiz ; li sires de Samtels et li sires de vientz Moley ; li sires de Mouceals et li sires de Pacie ; li séneschals de Corcye et li sires de Lacye ; li sires de Gacre et li sires Soillie ; li sires de Sacre ; li sires de Vaacre ; li sires de Torneor et li sires de Praerers ; William de Columbiers et Gilbert Dasmeres le Veil ; li sires de Chaaiones ; li sires de Coismieres le Veil ; Hugh de Bullebek ; Richard Orberk ; li sires de Bouesboz, et li sires de Sap ; li sires de Gloz et li sires de Tregoz ; li sires de Monfichet et Hugh Bigot ; li sires de Vitrie, et li sires Durmie ; li sires de Moubray et li sires de Saie ; li sires de la Fert et li sire Botenilam ; li sire Troselet et William Patrick de la Lande ; Monseir Hugh de Mortimer et li sires Damyler ; li sires de Dunebek et li sires de S. Clere et Robert Fitz Herveis, le quel fust occis en la bataille ; Tous ycels seigners desus nomé estoient à la retenaunce Monseir de Moion, si cum desus est diste.

II.

Et fait asavoir que toutes cestes gentez dount lor sor nouns y sont escritz vindrent ove William le Conquerour a de primes.

Aumarill et Deyncourt
Bertrem et Buttencourt
Biard et Biford
Bardolf et Basset
Deyville et Darcy
Pygot et Percy
Gurnay et Greilly
Tregos et Treylly
Camoys et Cameville
Hautein et Hauville
Warenne et Wauncy
Chauent et Chauncy
Loveyne et Lascy
Graunson et Tracy
Mohaud et Mooun

Bigot et Boown
Marny et Maundeville
Vipount et Umfreville
Morley et Moundeville
Baillof et Boundeville
Estraunge et Estoteville
Moubray et Morvile
Veer et Vinoun
Audel et Aungeloun
Vuasteneys et Waville
Soucheville Coudrey et Colleville
Fererers et Foleville
Briaunsoun et Baskeville
Neners et Nereville
Chaumberlayn et Chaumberoun

Fiz Walter et Werdoun
Argenteyn et Avenele
Ros et Ridel
Hasting et Haulley
Meneville et Mauley
Burnel et Buttevillain
Malebuche et Malemayn
Morteyne et Mortimer
Comyn et Columber
S. Cloyis et S. Clere
Otinel et S. Thomer
Gorgeise et Gower
Bruys et Dispenser
Lymesey et Latymer
Boys et Boteler
Fenes et Felebert
Fitz Roger et Fiz Robert
Muse et Martine
Quyncy et S. Quintine
Lungvilers et S. Ligiere
Griketot et Grevequer
Power et Panel, alias Paignel
Tuchet et Trusselle
Peche et Peverelle
Daubenay et Deverelle
Sainct Amande et Adryelle
Ryvers et Ryvel
Loveday et Lovel
Denyas et Druel
Mountburgh et Mounsorel
Maleville et Malet
Newmarch et Newbet
Corby. et Gorbet
Mounfey et Mounfichet
Gaunt et Garre
Maleberge et Marre
Geneville et Gifard
Someray et Howarde
Perot et Pykarde
Chaundoys et Chaward
Delahay et Haunsard

Mussegros et Musard
Maingun et Mountravers
Fovecourt et Feniers
Vescy et Verders
Brabasoun et Bevers
Challouns et Chaleys
Merkingfel et Mourreis
Fitz Philip et Fliot
Takel et Talbot
Lenias et Levecote
Tourbeville et Tipitot
Saunzauer et Saunford
Montagu et Mountfort
Forneux et Fournivaus
Valence et Vaus
Clerevalx et Clarel
Dodingle et Darel
Mautalent et Maudict
Chapes et Chaudut
Cauntelow et Coubray
Sainct Tese et Sauvay
Braund et Baybof
Fitz Alayne et Gilebof
Maunys et Meulos
Souley et Soules
Bruys et Burgh
Neville et Newburgh
Fitz William et Watervile
De Lalaund et de l'Isle
Sorel et Somery
S. John et S. Jory
Wavile et Warley
De la Pole et Pinkeney
Mortivaus et Mounthensy
Crescy et Courteny
S. Leo et Luscy
Bavent et Bussy
Lascels et Lovein
Thays et Tony
Hurel et Husee
Longvil et Longespe

De Wake et De la War
De la Marche et De la Marc
Constable et Tally
Poynce et Paveley
Tuk et Tany
Mallop et Marny
Paifrer et Plukenet
Bretonn et Blundet
Maihermer et Muschet
Baius et Bluet
Beke et Biroune
Saunz pour et Fitz Simoun
Gaugy et Gobaude
Rugetius et Fitz Rohaut
Peverel et Fitz Payne
Fitz Robert et Fitz Aleyne
Dakeny et Dautre
Menyle et Maufe
Maucovenaunt et Mounpinson
Pikard et Pinkadoun
Gray et Graunsoun
Diseney et Dabernoun
Maoun et Mainard
Banestre et Bekard
Bealum et Beauchaump
Loverak et Longchaump
Baudyn et Bray
Saluayn et Say
Ry et Rokel
Fitz Rafe et Rosel
Fitz Brian et Bracy
Playce et Placy
Damary et Deveroys
Vavasor et Warroys
Perpounte et Fitz Peris
Sesee et Solers
Nairmere et Fitz Nele
Waloys et Levele
Chaumpeneys et Chaunceus
Malebys et Mounceus
Thorny et Thornille

Wace et Wyvile
Verboys et Waceley
Pugoys et Paiteny
Galofer et Gubioun
Burdet et Boroun
Daverenge et Duylly
Sovereng et Suylly
Myriet et Morley
Tyriet et Turley
Fryville et Fressell
De la River et Rivel
Destraunges et Delatoun
Perrers et Pavillioun
Vallonis et Vernoun
Grymward et Geroun
Hercy et Heroun
Vendour et Veroun
Glauncourt et Chamount
Bawdewyn et Beaumont
Graundyn et Gerdoun
Blundet et Burdoun
Fitz-Rauf et Filiol
Fitz-Thomas et Tibol
Onatule et Cheyni
Mauliverer et Mouncy
Querru et Coingers
Mauclerk et Maners
Warde et Werlay
Musteys et Merlay
Barray et Bretevil
Tolimer et Treville
Blounte et Boseville
Liffard et Osevile
Benuy et Boyvile
Coursoun et Courtevile
Fitz-Morice et S. More
Broth et Barbedor
Fitz-Hugh et Fitz-Henry
Fitz-Arviz et Esturmy
Walangay et Fitzwarin
Fitz-Raynald et Roscelin

Baret et Bourte
Heryce et Harecourt
Venables et Venour
Hayward et Henour
Dulee et De la Laund
De la Valet et Veylaund
De la Plaunche et Puterel
Loring et Loterel
Fitz-Marmaduk et Mountrivel
Kymarays et Kyriel
Lisours et Longvale
Byngard et Bernevale
La Muile et Lownay
Damot et Damay
Bonet et Barry
Avenel et S. Amary
Jardyn et Jay
Tourys et Tay
Aimeris et Aveneris
Vilain et Valeris
Fitz Eustace et Eustacy
Mauches et Mascy
Brian et Bidin
Movet et S. Martine
Surdevale et Sengryn
Buscel et Bevery
Duraunt et Doreny
Disart et Doynell

Male Kake et Mauncel
Bernevile et Bretevile
Hameline et Hareville
De la Huse et Howel
Tingez et Gruyele
Tinel et Travile
Chartres et Chenil
Belew et Bertine
Mangysir et Mauveysin
Angers et Aungewyne
Tolet et Tisoun
Fermband et Frisoun
S. Barbe et Sageville
Vernoun et Waterville
Wemerlay et Wamervile
Broy et Bromevile
Bleyn et Breicourt
Tarteray et Chercourt
Oysel et Olifard
Maulovel et Maureward
Kanceis et Kevelers
Liof et Lymers
Rysers et Reynevil
Busard et Belevile
Rivers et Ripers
Percehay et Pereris
Fichent et Trivet

ANNOTATIONS.

Annotations.

In commencing these Annotations, we deem it right to observe that much doubt has been thrown upon the accuracy of the Roll of Battle Abbey, so far at least as it may be regarded as the Muster Roll of the Norman chiefs who survived the field of Hastings, there being more than suspicion that its holy guardians felt slight qualm at interpolation, when by that means they could propitiate the favour of some anticipated wealthy benefactor, or gratify the pride of some potent steel-clad baron. A recent writer endeavours, thus eloquently, to excuse the laxity of this celebrated record. "It was no unworthy pride," says Mr. Warburton,* "that would introduce a little of the Norman sap into the Family tree. And if to effect such an object, History be sometime twisted, and Heraldry suborned, let us look with indulgent eyes. Even at this day, in a country where titles command so much respect from the general worth of those who bear them, Norman Blood is the proudest boast, and Norman features the proudest distinction." The document is at all events one of monkish times, and has always been held in high estimation by the ancient chroniclers. Grafton calls the list he publishes, " The Names of the Gentlemen that came out of Normandy with William, Duke of that Prouynce, when he conquered the noble Realme of England: the which he states that he took out of an auncient Recorde that he had of Clarenceux King of Armes." And Stow asserts, that his Catalogue is transcribed from "A Table sometime in Battaille Abbey." Guilliam Tayleur, too, a Norman historian, who could not have had any communication with the monks of Battle, has given a copy of the Muster-Roll, according in most particulars with the list we have inserted.

The following details refer briefly to those soldiers of the conquest, of whom any authentic history remains, or from whom descendants may be traced. The information, meagre though it may be, will not be deemed valueless or uninteresting, by those through whose veins the Norman blood flows, and in whose breast the Norman spirit breathes. "On that soil," we again quote from Mr. Warburton's able work, "on that soil where they fixed their final home, the influences of Rollo and his race abide in monuments more enduring and worthier than Castles or Abbeys. In the skill that tames the war-horse—in the courage that 'rules the wave'— in the energies, the perseverance, the honour, the piety of the English people.

"Nor have those influences suffered diminution from the wear of eight hundred years. There is a vitality in the Norman spirit, on which time seems to have no power. Such as it was the day after Hastings, such is it now. Then it inspired the Norman Knight—it now breathes in the English Gentleman."

---
* ROLLO and HIS RACE, or Footsteps of the Normans, by Acton Warburton

AUMARLE, or ALBEMARLE.—This designation refers, in all probability, to Odo (brother-in-law of the Conqueror), who was styled D'Aumarle, from his possession of the city of Aumarle, in Normandy, which he held from the Archbishop of Rouen, on the condition that, in all expeditions where that Prelate went in person, he should be his standard-bearer, with twelve knights. After the battle of Hastings, Odo received a large share of the forfeited lands, among others, the lordship of Bytham in Lincolnshire, and the county or earldom of Holderness. He died in 1096. His grandson, William le Gros, third Earl of Albemarle, Chief Commander at the battle of the Standard, was rewarded for his gallantry on that occasion, with the Earldom of Yorkshire: he died in 1179, leaving two daughters, his coheirs, Hawyse, *m.* first, to William de Mandeville, Earl of Essex; and, secondly, to William de Fortibus; and Amicia *m.* to Eston.

AINCOURT.—The second name on the roll was that of a noble Norman, WALTER DE AINCOURT, who came from Aincourt, a lordship between Mantes and Magny, where the remains of the ancient family castle still exist. Walter was cousin of Remigius, Bishop of Lincoln, the munificent builder of Lincoln Cathedral, and obtained, as his share of the spoil, no less than sixty-seven lordships in several counties, chiefly in Lincolnshire, Blankney being the head of his feudal barony. The inscription on his son's tomb at Lincoln, whence it appears that he was connected by blood with the Royal family, thus describes him: "Hic jacet Wilhelmus filius Walteri Aiencuriensis, consanguinei Remigii Episcopi Lincolniensis, qui hanc ecclesiam fecit.—Præfatus Wilhelmus, regiâ stirpe progenitus, dum in curiâ Wilhelmi filii magni Regis Wilhelmi qui Angliam conquisivit aleretur III Kalend. Novemb. obiit." RALPH D'EYNCOURT, Walter's second son, and brother of this William, founded Thurgarton Priory, Notts, and was a great feudal baron of his time. From him derived, in the sixth degree, EDMUND, BARON D'EYNCOURT, who had immense possessions, and in the reigns of Edward I. and Edward II. acted a conspicuous part in most of the stirring events of the period. His two sons, John and William, who were with the feudal army at Carlisle, 29 Edward I., figure in the Roll of Carlaverock, where John, it is said, *mult bien fist son devoir*. He died in his father's lifetime, and subsequently his brother William, a commander of renown, was killed before the castle of Stirling, on the eve of the battle of Bannockburn, an event referred to by Sir Walter Scott in the "Lord of the Isles:"—

"Back to the host the Douglas rode,
And soon glad tidings are abroad,
That D'Eyncourt by stout Randolph slain,
His followers fled with loosen'd rein."

At the decease of Baron Edmund the title devolved on his grandson, William, 9th Lord of D'Eyncourt, an eminent warrior who participated in the glorious achievements of the reign of Edward III. He was one of the commanders at the famous battle of Neville's Cross in 1346, and was at the head of the guard attendant on Queen Philippa previous to that conflict. To him also was consigned the custody of John, King of France, taken prisoner at Poictiers, and he finally conducted that monarch out of Lincolnshire (where he had been in Lord D'Eyncourt's charge) to the Metropolis, at the period of his release in 1364, when King Edward himself attended him to the coast, and the Black Prince to Calais. But we will not attempt in these annotations to follow the fortunes of this gallant and pre-eminently distinguished race; suffice it to add, that the eventual heiress, ALICE BARONESS D'EYNCOURT, and also Baroness Grey of Rotherfield, born in 1404, married for her first husband, William, Baron Lovell and Holland, and had by him two sons, JOHN, Lord Lovell and Holland, and William Lord Morley, "jure uxoris, Alianoræ, filiæ Roberti, Dom. de Morley." The former, John, Lord Lovell and Holland, died before his mother, 4 Edward IV., leaving with two daughters an only son, FRANCIS, Lord Lovell and Holland, who became also by maternal inheritance, Baron D'Eyncourt, and Grey of Rotherfield, and by creation Viscount Lovel. True to the House of York, he fought for Richard III. at Bosworth, and subsequently took part, in 1487, in the Battle of Stoke, where he escaped by swimming the Trent on horseback, and is said to have lain hid for many years in a cave or vault. Lord Bacon mentions this report, and in 1708, a skeleton, supposed to be that of Lord Lovel and D'Eyncourt, was discovered in a concealed room in his castle of Minster Lovel, sitting at a table, with a book, paper, pen, &c. before him, and in another part of the room lay a cap, all much mouldered and decayed. Hence it may be concluded that this once powerful but unhappy lord retired secretly to his own castle, and having entrusted himself to some friend or dependent, died either by treachery or neglect, or in consequence of some accident befalling that person. By attainder, 11 Henry VII., fell the ancient barony of D'Eyncourt with his other honours and vast estates, and amongst them, the manors of Bayons and Tevilby, co. Lincoln, which became by subsequent grant and re-purchase, the property of the Tennyson family, and the former is now the stately residence of the Right Hon. Charles Tennyson D'Eyncourt, who descends from the heir of this distinguished nobleman, namely, William, second son of Alice, Baroness D'Eyncourt and Grey.

AUDELEY.—We apprehend that this name was an interpolation by the monks; for Dugdale asserts that it arose in the time of King John, and was then first assumed from territorial possessions, by a branch of that ancient and noble family of

Verdon, whose chief seat was at Alton Castle, in the northern part of Staffordshire. In the immediately succeeding reigns few families held a more conspicuous place in history, but its most distinguished member was the renowned James de Audley, Lord Audley, the hero of Poictiers. With his son and successor, Nicholas, Lord Audley, summoned to parliament from 1387 to 1390, the male line of this illustrious house expired, but the barony devolved on the grandson of his lordship's sister, Joane Touchet, and is still enjoyed by her representative.

ANGUILLIAM, or AGUILLON.—In Gibson's "Camden's Britannia," it is stated that Sir Robert Aguillon had a castle at the manor of Addington, in Surrey, which was holden in fee by the serjeantcy, to find in the king's kitchen, on the coronation day, a person to make a dainty dish called "Mapiger noun, or Dillegrout," and serve the same up to the king's table. This service has been regularly claimed by the lords of the said manor, and allowed at the respective coronations of the kings of England. Isabel, the daughter and heiress of Robert Aguillon, m. Hugh, Baron Bardolf.

ARGENTINE.—The descendants of this Norman chieftain, David de Argentine, became feudal barons of great personal distinction. Reginald de Argentine, who appears to have been fifth in descent from the companion in arms of the Conqueror, succeeded to all his father Giles de Argentine's vast estates, including the manor of Great Wymondeley, in Cambridgeshire, holden by grand serjeantie, "to serve the king upon the day of his coronation with a silver cup;" and was summoned to parliament as a baron, 25 Edward I. Of the same ancestry was Reginald de Argentine, who, in the 21 Henry III. being a knight templar, was standard bearer of the Christian army in a great battle against the Turks, near Antioch, wherein he was slain; and Sir Giles de Argentine, who so gallantly fell at Bannockburn. This accomplished knight had served in the wars of Henry of Luxemburgh with such high reputation, that he was, in popular estimation, the third worthy of the age. Those to whom fame assigned precedence, were Henry of Luxemburgh himself, and Robert Bruce. Argentine had warred in Palestine, encountered thrice with the Saracens, and had slain two antagonists in each engagement; an easy matter, he said, for one Christian knight to slay two Pagan dogs. His death corresponded with his life. In conjunction with Aymer de Valence, Earl of Pembroke, he was appointed to attend immediately upon the person of Edward II. at Bannockburn. When the day was utterly lost, they forced the king from the field. De Argentine saw Edward safe from danger, and then took his leave of him. "God be with you, Sire," he said, "it is not my wont to fly." With this expression he turned his horse, cried his war-cry, plunged into the midst of the combatants, and was slain.

> "And O farewell!" the victor cried,
> "Of chivalry the flower and pride,
> The arm in battle bold,
> The courteous mien, the noble race,
> The stainless faith, the manly face!—
> Bid Ninian's convent light their shrine,
> For late-wake of De Argentine;
> O'er better knight on death bier laid,
> Torch never gleamed nor mass was said."

ARUNDEL.—According to Domesday Book, Roger de Arundel was found to be possessed of twenty-eight lordships in Somerset, 20 William the Conqueror, and he, no doubt, was the Norman whose name appears on the roll. From him sprang the great western family of Arundel, so distinguished under its branches of Lanherne, Wardour, and Trerice.

AVENANT, OR D'AVENANT —This Norman family settled in Essex, and styled their chief seat Davenant. One of the descendants was John Davenant, Bishop of Salisbury. Their *Arms* were, *Gu. three escallops erm. between eight cross crosslets fitchée or.*

ABELL was also an Essex family, although branches spread into the counties of Kent and Derby. An entry regarding them occurs in the Visitation of the latter county, A.D. 1611. Their *Arms* were, *Arg. a saltire engr. az.*

AUNWERS, OR D'ANVERS.—This name, taken from the town of Anvers, was borne by Roland D'Anvers, who came thence to the conquest of England. He was ancestor of the families of D'Anvers of Culworth, raised to the degree of baronets in 1642, of D'Anvers of Dantsey, ennobled under the title of Danby, and D'Anvers of Horley.

ARCHER.—Fulbert L'Archer, the patriarch of the Lords Archer of Umberslade, in the co. of Warwick, appears among the warriors at Hastings, who received recompense from the victor. His son, Robert L'Archer, obtained additions to his territorial possessions by grant from Henry I., whose tutor he had been, and still further increased his patrimony by marrying Sebit, daughter of Henry de Villiers, and thus acquiring the lands of Umberslade. During the wars of the Plantagenets, the Archers were much distinguished, and for a long series of generations held a leading position in the county of Warwick. The last male heir, Andrew Archer, second Lord Archer, of Umberslade, nineteenth in direct descent from the Norman L'Archer, died in 1778, leaving four daughters and coheirs, Catherine, married first, to Other Lewis, fourth Earl of Plymouth, and secondly, to William, first Earl of Amherst; Elizabeth, married to Christopher Musgrave, Esq.; Henrietta, married to Edward Bolton Clive, Esq., of Whitfield; and Maria, married to Henry Howard, Esq., of Corby Castle.

ARCY, or D'ARCY.—From an ancient and most valuable pedigree compiled by Camden, now in the possession of John D'Arcy, Esq., of Hyde Park, co. Westmeath, it appears that

Norman D'Arcy, the progenitor of the great baronial house of D'Arcy, was amongst the most liberally rewarded of the Conqueror's followers. He received by the immediate gift of William, no less than thirty-three lordships in Lincolnshire, of which Nocton became for divers after ages the chief seat of his descendants.

ALBENY.—William de Albini, surnamed *Pincerna*, son of Roger de Albini, and elder brother of Nigel de Albini, whose posterity, under the name of Mowbray, attained such eminence in after ages, accompanied the Duke of Normandy to England, and acquired extensive estates by royal grants in the county of Norfolk and elsewhere; of which was the lordship of Bokenham, to be holden by the service of being butler to the kings of England on the day of their coronation. William de Albini, a munificent benefactor to the church, founded the abbey of Wymundham, in Norfolk, and bestowed his lands in Stavell, on the church of St. Etienne, at Caen, in Normandy. His son and heir, William de Albini, was surnamed "William with the Strong Hand," from a gallant achievement performed by him at a tournament at Paris, and quaintly related by Dugdale in his Baronage. He subsequently obtained the hand of the Queen Adeliza, relict of King Henry I., and daughter of GODFREY, DUKE OF LORRAINE, which Adeliza had the CASTLE of ARUNDEL in dowry from the deceased monarch, and thus her new lord became its feudal earl. With this potent noble's grandson, HUGH DE ALBINI, fourth Earl, who died *s.p.* in 1243, this branch of the great house of Albini expired, while its large possessions devolved upon the earl's sisters as coheiresses: thus Mabel, the eldest, married to Robert de Tateshall, had the castle and manor of Buckenham; Isabel, the second, married to John Fitzalan, Baron of Clun and Oswestry, had the castle and manor of Arundel, which conveyed the earldom to her husband; Nicola, the third, married to Roger de Somery, had the manor of Barwe, in Leicestershire; and Cecilie, the fourth, married to Roger de Montalt, had the castle of Rising, in Norfolk.

BERTRAM.—William de Bertram, the son or grandson of the Norman soldier, founded the Augustinian Priory of Brinkburn, in Northumberland. His descendants—the Bertrams of Mitford castle, were potent feudal lords, distinguished in the Scottish wars and baronial contests. The last male heir, Roger Bertram, second Baron Bertram, died in 1311, leaving an only daughter, Agnes, at whose decease without issue, the Barony of Bertram of Mitford, fell into abeyance between her ladyship's cousins and coheirs, and so continues amongst their representatives. Those coheirs were William Fitzwilliam of Sprotborough, Philip D'Arcy, Elias de Penulbury, and Gilbert de Aton.

BUTTSCOURT.—This was meant probably for BOTETOURT, the name of an old Norman race, whose descendants were summoned to parliament as barons in the reigns of the first three Edwards. At the death of John, Lord Botetourt, in 1335, Joyce, Lady Burnell, his granddaughter, became his sole heiress, but that lady dying *s.p.* in 1406, the Barony of Botetourt fell into abeyance between her aunts, and so continued among their descendants for more than three centuries and a half, when it was at length called out in favour of the representative of Katherine de Berkeley, and is now vested in the Duke of Beaufort.

BARDOLF.—This occurrence of the name is the only indication we have of the Norman founder of the Bardolfs, the first of whom on record is William Bardulf, who served as sheriff of Norfolk and Suffolk, *temp.* Henry II. In the succeeding reign, Doun Bardolf, the grandson of the sheriff, acquired in marriage with Beatrix, daughter and heiress of William de Warren, the Barony of Wirmegay in Norfolk, and thenceforth Wirmegay became the designation of the family. Another fortunate alliance, that of John, third Lord Bardolf, a banneret of the martial time of Edward III., with the daughter and coheiress of Sir Roger D'Amorie, still further augmented the possessions of the house, but all were lost at the death and attainder of the fifth and ill-fated lord, who, joining the Earl of Northumberland's insurrection, was mortally wounded at Bramham Moor. His daughters and coheirs were Anne, married first to Sir William Clifford, Knt., and secondly to Reginald, Lord Cobham; and Joane, married to Sir William Phelip, K.G.

BASSET.—In the Conqueror's survey, Thurstan, a Norman, held six hides of land in Drayton, co. Stafford, and this Thurstan, according to Dugdale, was paternal ancestor of the several families of Basset, which rose into power and distinction very shortly after the Conquest. Ralph Basset, the illustrious founder of their greatness, is said (Ordericus Vitalis) to have been raised by Henry I. from a lowly condition, and to have been " exalted above earls and other eminent men." True it is he was constituted Justice of England, and invested with the power of sitting in whatever court he pleased, and where he might list, for the administration of justice; but it is not equally certain that he was of so humble an origin, for we find his son, in the reign of Stephen, "abounding in wealth, and erecting a strong castle upon some part of his *inheritance* in Normandy." The son having such an heritable property, would clearly indicate that the family was of importance in the Dukedom, prior to the conquest of England, and strongly supports the assertion of the Battell Abbey Roll, that its patriarch in this country came over with the Conqueror. It is not, however, of much consequence, for Ralph Basset required none of the artificial aids of ancestry to attain distinction. A lawgiver, a statesman, and an unsullied judge, he had within himself powers sufficient at any period to reach the goal of honour, but particularly in the rude age in which he lived. Of his descendants, we may enumerate the Lords Basset of Weldon, the Lords Basset of Drayton, the Lords Basset of Sapcoate, the Bassets of Umberleigh, in Devon, and the Bassets of Tehidy.

BRABAZON.—The family of Barbanzon, Brabazon, or Brabanzon, assumed their surname from the Castle of Brabazon, in Normandy, whence JAQUES LE BRABASON (called the Great Warrior) came to the aid of William of Normandy in his conquest of England, and consequently appears in the list of Battle Abbey. JOHN LE BRABASON, son of the Norman, fixed his residence at Betchworth, in Surrey, and was living in the reigns of Henry I. and Henry II. From him derived the Brabazons of Eastwell, in Leicestershire, of whom was John le Brabazon, of Eastwell, slain at the Battle of Bosworth. His grandson, SIR WILLIAM BRABAZON, of Eastwell, Lord Treasurer and Lord Chief Justice of Ireland, died in 1552, leaving by Elizabeth his wife, daughter and coheir of Nicholas Clifford, Esq., of Holme, in Kent (great grandson and heir male of Sir Lewis Clifford, K.G.,) two sons,—I. SIR EDWARD BRABAZON, first Lord Ardee, ancestor of the Earls of Meath, of the Brabazons of Rath House, co. Louth, and of the Brabazons of Tara House, county Meath; and II. of SIR ANTHONY BRABAZON, of Ballinasloe Castle, Governor of Connaught, ancestor of the Brabazons of Brabazon Park, co. Mayo, whose last male representative, Sir William John Brabazon, Bart., died in 1840, leaving his nephew, William John Sharpe, Esq., of Oaklands, Sussex (afterwards Brabazon), his heir.

BASKERVILLE.—The family of Baskerville is one of the most ancient and honourable in England, and from the time of its Norman patriarch, has continued to hold the highest position amongst the great landed proprietors. Its earliest residence was the castle of Erdisley in Herefordshire, and among the first knightly ancestors of the race we may mention Sir Robert Baskerville of Erdisley, whose wife was Agnes, daughter and heiress of Nesta, daughter of Rees ap Griffith, Prince of South Wales; Sir Richard Baskerville, who represented the county of Hereford in parliament in 1295; and Sir John Baskerville of Combe, who served in the retinue of Henry V. at the battle of Agincourt. At a later period Sir Thomas Baskerville of Goodrest, in Warwickshire, commanded, as general, the English army in Picardy. The heiress of the chief line, Eleanor Baskerville, married John Talbot of Grafton, Esq., and was mother of John, 16th Earl of Shrewsbury; several junior branches established themselves in various counties, and in all sustained the honour of the name; the Baskervilles, Lords of Lawton and Pickthorne, county Salop; the Baskervilles of Netherwood, of Goodrest, and of Aberedow and Lambedr. The late male representative, Lieut.-Col. THOMAS BASKERVILLE, who died *s. p.* in 1817, devised his estates to his cousin, the present THOMAS BASKERVILLE MYNORS-BASKERVILLE, Esq., of Clyrow, M.P. for Herefordshire, younger brother of Peter Rickards-Mynors, Esq., of Treago. Mr. Baskerville derives, from the Aberedow line, through his grandmother, Philippa, wife of the Rev. John Powell, and daughter and heir of Thomas Baskerville, Esq.

BOTELER.—This name originated from the office of boteler or butler, held by its founder. The Botelers, potent feudal barons from the time of the first Plantagenets, were frequently summoned to parliament. The heiress of William, Lord Boteler, of Wemme, married for her first husband, Sir Robert Ferrers, and from this alliance sprang the Lords Ferrers of Wemme.

BOURCHIER.—Of the early history of this illustrious house from the era of its Norman patriarch to the time of the second Edward, we know nothing; but in the reign of that monarch, Sir JOHN DE BOURCHIER became one of the judges of the Court of King's Bench, and acquired in marriage the lordship of Stansted in Essex. His son, ROBERT DE BOURCHIER, constituted (14 Edward III.) Lord Chancellor of England, united the civic and military characters, and was gallantly distinguished in arms, particularly at the battle of Cressy. This eminent person left two sons, John, second Lord Bourchier, whose line soon became extinct, and William, whose son William Earl of Ewe, in Normandy, married Anne Plantagenet, daughter and sole heiress of Thomas of Woodstock, Duke of Gloucester, son of Edward III., and had issue—1. Henry Earl of Ewe and Essex; 2. Thomas Archbishop of Canterbury; 3. William Lord Fitzwarine; 4. John Lord Berners; and 5. Anne, consort of John Mowbray, Duke of Norfolk. The eldest of the sons, Henry Earl of Ewe and Essex, Lord Treasurer of England, was grandfather of Henry, the second and last Earl of Essex, a gallant courtier of his day, and captain of Henry the Eighth's body guard, who attended his royal master into France as Lieut.-General of all the Spears: and at the famous tournament which Henry held in the eighth year of his reign, the Earl of Essex, with the King himself, the Duke of Suffolk, and Nicholas Carew, answered all comers. A few years after, his lordship again attended his sovereign to France, and swelled the pageantry upon the field of the Cloth of Gold. The Earl died in consequence of a fall from his horse in 1539, and his barony of Bourchier was eventually inherited by the descendants of his sister Cicely, wife of John Devereux, Lord Ferrers of Chartley, and they became also by creation Earls of Essex.

BERNERS.—Margery, daughter and heir of Richard Berners, of West Horsely, in Surrey, commonly called

Lord Berners, the descendant of the Norman knight, married Sir John Bourchier, K. G., fourth son of William, Earl of Ewe, by Anne Plantagenet, his wife, and her husband was summoned to Parliament from 1455 to 1472, as "John Bourchier de Berners, Chevalier." The title thus created, fell into abeyance, and descending through heiresses, to Robert Wilson, Esq., of Didlington, and Mrs. Louisa Strangwayes, as co-heirs, was eventually conferred on the former.

BOHUN.—Of Humphrey de Bohun, the warrior whose name occurs on the Roll, little more has been ascertained than that he became possessed of the lordship of Taterford, in Norfolk, and that he was a near kinsman of the Conqueror. His son and successor, Humphrey de Bohun, surnamed the Great, married, by command of William Rufus, Maud, daughter of Edward de Saresbury, and thus acquired considerable estates in Wiltshire; but the greatness of the Bohuns arose from the marriage of his son, Humphrey de Bohun, steward to Henry I., with Margery, daughter and eventual coheir of Milo de Gloucester, Earl of Hereford, Lord High Constable of England. Thenceforward the high and dignified office of High Constable of the Realm vested in the Bohuns, and shortly after the Earldom of Hereford was conferred on Henry de Bohun by King John. That nobleman's son, Humphrey de Bohun, Earl of Hereford, inheriting the honour of Essex from his mother, Maud, sister and heiress of William de Mandeville, last Earl of Essex, was created Earl of that county by Henry III., and in a few years after stood sponsor for Prince Edward. In 1250, he assumed the cross, and proceeded to the Holy Land, and in the great contest between the King and the Barons, fought under the banner of the latter, in whose army his son Humphrey was one of the most distinguished leaders, and commanded the infantry at the Battle of Evesham. Although strongly tempted by the heroism and pre-eminent services of this illustrious race, to dwell more at length on their history, we are compelled by our limited space to confine ourselves to a mere mention of their extinction. Humphrey de Bohun, the last Earl of Hereford, Northampton and Essex, did not long enjoy his great accumulation of honour, for he died in 1372, in the 32d year of his age, leaving by Joane his wife, daughter of the Earl of Arundel, two daughters, his coheirs, viz., Alianore, married to Thomas of Woodstock, Duke of Gloucester, sixth son of Edward III., and Mary, married to Henry, Earl of Derby, created in 1397, Duke of Hereford. The latter all-potent noble, son of John of Gaunt "time-honored Lancaster," ascended the throne of England as Henry IV.

BONDEVILLE.—The descendant of this Norman chief was summoned to Parliament, 28 Henry VI., as Baron Bonville of Chuton. He subsequently espoused the interests of the House of York, and was one of those to whom the custody of Henry VI. was committed after the Battle of Northampton; the tide of fortune, however, turning, his Lordship lost his head after the second Battle of St. Alban's, and as his grandson and heir apparent William, commonly called Lord Harrington, had fallen previously on the hard-fought field of Wakefield, Lord Bonville was succeeded by his great-granddaughter, Cecily Bonville, who married first Thomas Grey, Marquis of Dorset, and secondly, Henry Stafford, Earl of Wiltshire.

BANASTRE.—This name, as we are told by Camden (*Remains*), was probably a title of office, which he latinizes Balneator. The derivation is not improbable, as we find an ancient coat assigned to the name in one of the Lancashire visitations, with the principal charge *a water bouget*. A pedigree of the chief line of this family, from its founder down to the time of Edward I., has been preserved in a petition on the rolls of parliament. It appears from this document and other historical evidence, that Robert Banastre who came over with King William, held the lordship of Prestatyn, one of the hundreds of Flintshire, under Robert of Rhudlau (de Rodelent), a kinsman of the Conqueror. Here a tower was built on the coast, whereof the foundations are still discoverable. It was destroyed by the Welsh in the time of Henry II., when they regained possession of that district. At this time Robert, the son of Robert Banastre, withdrew with all his people into Lancashire, where the clan appear to have been long known by the denomination of "Les Westrays" (*v. Rot. Parl.*), and where they are found holding extensive possessions under the Earls of Chester, whose Palatinate extended over the south of that county. Thurstan Banastre, son of the second Robert, inherited the barony of Newton, in Makerfield, a district which in Domesday Survey ranks as a separate hundred, though it has since merged in that of West Derby. He also held the lordship of Walton in the Dale, under the Lacys, Lords of Mackburnshire, and Mollington-Banastre, near Chester, &c., &c. The latter estate passed by marriage of a daughter to the Hoghtons, the superiority remaining with the Banastres and their representatives. The barony of Newton and the lordship of Walton le Dale came to the Langtons by the marriage of Alice (daughter of James, and granddaughter and heir to Robert Banastre, the descendant of Thurstan), with John, son of Robert de Langeton, in the county of Leicester, brother to John de Langeton, Lord Chancellor in the time of Edward I.*

The honours of the Banastres continued for about three hundred

---

* This Chancellor has been erroneously assigned by Lord Campbell to the family of Langton in Lincolnshire.

years in the family of Langton. The last baron of that name, who was a Knight of the Bath at the coronation of James I., ceded Walton to the Hoghtons of Hoghton Tower, in consequence of a fatal feud with that family, in which its head had fallen, and as he died without issue, the fee of Makerfeld went by heir female to the Fleetwoods, from whom it was inherited by the Leghs of Lyme. The representative of the family in the male line is Jos. Langton, Esq., of Liverpool.

Mr. Beltz, in his "Memorials of the Order of the Garter," has traced the descent of a collateral branch of the Lancashire Banastres, from whom sprang one of the early knights of that order: but he falls into a singular mistake when relating the first settlement of the family at Prestatyn, in Englefield, by fixing Englefield in Berkshire, whereas it was the ancient name of that portion of the original earldom of Chester, now known as Flintshire. From the same division of the clan which furnished the Knight of the Garter, sprang the Banastres of Bank. They are now represented by R. Townley Parker, Esq., of Cuerden, but their manor of Bretherton is in other hands.

These branches of the family bore for arms, *a cross flory sable on a field argent*, which cognizance was quartered by the Langtons (*v. Visitation*), along with *argent three chevrons gules*, a coat which they also inherited from their predecessors in the barony of Newton, as is proved by its use in sealing deeds by the last baron of the name of Banastre. The paternal coat of Langton was *argent an eagle displayed with two heads vert.*

BRAIBUF.—This name occurs in the Hampshire Visitation of 1634, wherein it is recorded that the daughter and heiress of Sir Hugh Braybuff married Sir John Hamlyn, Knt., and had an only child, who became the wife of Sir Hugh Conway and the mother of a daughter and heiress, who wedded Thomas Tame, and left a daughter and heiress, Catherine, married to John Whithed, Esq., of Titherley, Hants.

BOIS.—From an ancient and valuable pedigree, prepared by John Boys, Esq., of Margate, it appears that this Norman Bois, or John de Bois, or de Bosco, was the progenitor of the East Kent Boys's, who are described by Phillpot in his Villare Paulianum, 1659, as a "numerous and knightley familie," and as "having been settled for seventeen prior descents at Bonyngton." One of the descendants, Colonel John Boys was governor of Donnington Castle, in Berkshire, in 1644, and was knighted by King Charles, for his gallant defence of that castle against the rebels, and received an augmentation to his bearing of a crown imperial or on a canton az. Sir John Boys, of St. Gregories, Canterbury, founded Jesus Hospital there in 1612. The lineage of the East Kent Boys's is in the Supplemental Volume of Burke's "*Landed Gentry.*"

BURGH.—Robert de Burgh, Earl of Moreton in Normandy, son of Harlowen de Burgh, by Arlotta, his wife, mother of William the Conqueror, participated with his half-brother in the triumph at Hastings, was created Earl of Cornwall, and received, as a further recompense, grants of seven hundred and ninety-three manors. This potent noble left one son, William Earl of Cornwall, who, rebelling against the first HENRY, joined Robert of Normandy, and led the van at the battle of Tenchebray. In this conflict, after displaying great personal valour, he fell into the hands of his opponents and was sent prisoner to England, where he was treated with much cruelty, the king causing his eyes to be put out, and detaining him in captivity for life. The period of the Earl's death is not recorded, but Lodge (*Peerage of Ireland*, Vol. I.) states that the ill-fated nobleman left two sons—I. Adelm, from whom descended the Burghs, Earls of Ulster, the noble House of Clanricarde, and the various families of Burke, so widely scattered over the south west district of Ireland: and II. John, whose son, Hubert de Burgh, Earl of Kent, was Justiciary of England, *temp.* Henry III., and one of the greatest subjects in England.*

* Hubert de Burgh married, 1st, Joan, daughter of William de Vernun, Earl of Devon; 2nd, Beatrix, daughter of William de Warren, of Wermgay, in Norfolk; 3rd, Isabel, daughter and coheir of William Earl of Gloucester; and 4th, Margaret, daughter of William, King of Scotland. His lordship had issue a son, SIR HUBERT DE BURGH, whose son, WILLIAM DE BURGH, summoned to Parliament 1st of Edward III., had, with an elder son JOHN, ancestor of the LORDS BURGH of Gainsborough, a younger son SIR HUGH DE BURGH, Knt., who married Elizabeth, sole daughter and heiress of Foulk, Lord of Mawddwy in Merioneth, grandson of William, (living 17 Edward I.) fourth son of Griffith ap Gwenwynwyn, Prince of Powys Wenwynwyn, and was father of a son and heir, SIR JOHN DE BURGH, Knt., Lord of Mawddwy, who married Joan, daughter and coheir of Sir William Clopton, Knt. of Clopton, co. Warwick, and Radbrook, co. Gloucester, and had issue four daughters and coheirs—I. Elizabeth, married Thomas Newport, Esq., of High Ercall, ancestor of the extinct Earls of Bradford, and their descendants in the female line, the present EARL OF BRADFORD; II. Ancreda, married John Leighton, Esq., of Stratton, and *jure uxoris* of Watlesboro', ancestor of the present SIR BALDWIN LEIGHTON, Bart. of Watlesboro' and Loton Park; III. Isabel, married Sir John Lingeyn, Knt. of Lingeyn, and *jure uxoris*, of Radbrook, ancestor of Robert Lingen, Esq., of Sutton Court, Herefordshire and Radbrook, who assumed the name of BURTON, and was father of ROBERT BURTON, Esq., of Longnor-Hall and of Radbrook; IV. Eleanor, married Thomas Mytton, Esq., M.P. for Shrewsbury in 1472, *jure uxoris*, Lord of the Barony of Mawddwy, ancestor of, I. The MYTTONS OF HALSTON; II. MYTTONS OF

BLUAT.—The descendants of this Norman knight were at an early period Lords of Ragland. One branch became seated in the county of Devon, and acquired Holcombe Rogus in the 15th century, by the marriage of John Bluett with a co-heiress of Chiselden. The great grandson of this alliance, Richard Bluett, Esq., of Holcombe, had two sons—Sir Roger Bluett, Knt., who died in 1566, and was ancestor of the BLUETTS of Devon; and Francis, from whom sprang the Bluetts of Cornwall.

BRAIOUS.—One of the most distinguished commanders in the army of the Conqueror—if we can judge from the broad lands he acquired in the counties of Berks, Wilts, Surrey, Dorset and Sussex—was WILLIAM DE BRAOSE, a noble Norman, who held, in his native Duchy, the Honour of Braose near Falaise. His son, PHILIP DE BRAOSE, much increased his inheritance by marrying Berta, sister and co-heir of William, Earl of Gloucester, receiving with her the rich Lordship of Brecknock and other extensive estates. The issue of the marriage was two sons; the elder, WILLIAM DE BRAOSE, a feudal lord of great sway and influence, obtained from Henry II. a grant of the "whole kingdom of Limerick in Ireland," for the service of sixty knights' fees, and continuing during the two succeeding reigns to bask in the sunshine of royal favour, he considerably augmented his power and possessions. Finally, however, he experienced in an especial degree the proverbial inconstancy of kingly smiles, and had to fly from England to escape the anger of King John. Various accounts of the cause of Braose's disgrace have been handed down—some ascribing it to his refusal to give hostages to the jealous monarch, in proof of his allegiance, while others consider his banishment a just punishment for the cruelties inflicted by himself and his wife, Lady Maud de St. Waleric, on the Welsh people. Dubious though this point may be, certain it is that the most melancholy fate awaited the fallen lord and his family. In the year 1240, according to Matthew of Westminster, "the noble lady, Maud, wife of William de Braose, with William, their son and heir, were miserably famished at Windsore, by the command of King John; and William, her husband,

---

GARTH AND PENYLAN; III. MUTTON (SIR PETER) OF LLANERCH PARK, co. Denbigh, whose daughter and coheir, Anne Mutton, of Llanerch Park, married Robert Davies, Esq., of Gwysaney, co. Flint, and from this marriage derived the DAVIES's of Gwysaney and the late Thomas Davies, Esq., of Trefynant, co. Denbigh, father of OWEN DAVIES, Esq., of Eton House, co. Kent, and of Elizabeth Davies, m. to the late William Hughes, Esq., of Pen-y-clawdd, male representative of Hughes of Gwerclas.

escaping from Scorham, put himself into the habit of a beggar, and privately getting beyond sea, died soon after at Paris, where he had burial in the Abbey of St. Victor." William de Braose had, by Maud, his wife, four daughters:—Joan, married to Richard, Lord Percy; Loretta, married to Robert Fitz-Parnell, Earl of Leicester; Margaret, married to Walter de Lacy; and Maud, married to Griffith, Prince of South Wales; and four sons, viz., 1, William, who perished by starvation at Windsor, leaving a son John, grandfather of William, Lord Braose, of Gower, whose barony is now in abeyance among the descendants of his daughters and co-heirs, Aliva de Moubray and Joan de Bohun; 2, Giles, Bishop of Hereford; 3, Reginald of Bergavenny, who fell a victim to the jealousy of Llewelyn, Prince of Wales, and was seized and put to death. He left four daughters:—Isabel, married to David ap Llewelyn, and secondly to Peter Fitzherbert; Maud, married to Roger, Lord Mortimer; Eve, married to William de Cantelupe; and Eleanor, married to Humphrey de Bohun. 4, John (Sir), who had from his father the manor of Knill, in the marches of Wales, and thence adopting the surname of Knill, became ancestor of the Knills of Knill, now represented by Sir John Walsham, Bart., of Knill.

BROWNE.—This ancient and widespreading name, which occurs in early writings in a great variety of forms, as Le Brun, de Bron, Broun, Brune, Brunn, &c., stands 50th on the Battle Roll, and has the peculiar distinction of having produced twenty-one different families in the United Kingdom, who have received from the Sovereign hereditary titles of Nobility. Of these, only six exist. In England, the great house of Browne, Viscount Montague, and the Brownes of Walcot, Beechworth Castle, and Kiddington, Baronets, have all become extinct: but in Scotland, the Brouns of Colstoun have still a male representative. Their ancestor, Gualterus le Brun, Baron of Colstoun, appears, on the parchment roll of the See of Glasgow, as one of the witnesses to the inquisition made by Prince David, in 1116, the oldest Scottish document extant. The late Countesses of Dalhousie and Carnwath were of the Colstoun family; nor, amongst the numerous female descendants of the race, who have shed lustre on the name, are we to forget two, ever dear and memorable —the late sweet songstress, Mrs. Hemans, and the mother of the immortal poet, Burns. In Ireland, the Lords Sligo, Kenmare, Kilmaine, and Oranmore, all claim descent from the Norman chieftain.

BEKE.—The lordship of Eresby, in Lincolnshire, was settled by William the Conqueror, with other manors, upon Walter de Bec, one of the most distinguished knights at Hastings. By Agnes, his wife, daughter and heiress of Hugh Dapifer, Walter left, with other issue, a son, HENRY BEKE, of Eresby, great

great grandfather of WALTER BEKE, whose three sons were John, Lord Beke, of Eresby; Anthony, Bishop of Durham, Patriarch of Jerusalem; and Thomas, Bishop of St. David's. Of these, the eldest, John, Lord Beke, died in 1302, leaving one son, Walter, who had no issue, and two daughters—Alice, married to Sir William de Willoughby, Knt., ancestor, by her, of the present Lord Willoughby de Eresby; and Margaret, married to Sir Richard de Harcourt, progenitor of the Earls of Harcourt. Anthony Beke, the famous Bishop of Durham, was one of the most illustrious men in history. Amongst his other works, he founded the collegiate churches of Chester and Langcester, as well as the chapel at Bishop Auckland, all in the county palatine of Durham. "Moreover," says Dugdale, "it is reported that no man in all the realm, except the king, did equal him for habit, behaviour, and military pomp; and that he was more versed in state affairs than in ecclesiastical duties; ever assisting the king most powerfully in his wars, having sometimes in Scotland twenty-six standard bearers, and of his ordinary retinue an hundred and forty knights; so that he was thought to be rather a temporal prince than a priest or bishop; and lastly, that he died on 3rd of March, 1310, and was buried above the High Altar in his cathedral of Durham."

BEAUCHAMPE.—Hugh de Beauchampe, the Norman, obtained grants to a very great extent, from the Conqueror after the Battle of Hastings; and appears at the general survey to have been possessed of large estates in the counties of Hertford, Buckingham, and Bedford. His direct descendant, in the 7th degree, WILLIAM DE BEAUCHAMP, Lord of Elmley, who succeeded to the earldom of Warwick, in right of his mother Isabel, sister and heiress of William Manduit, Earl of Warwick, died in 1298, leaving, with several daughters, one son, GUY DE BEAUCHAMP, Earl of Warwick, who acquired high military reputation in the martial times of the first Edward, distinguishing himself at the Battle of Falkirk, at the Siege of Calaverock, and upon different occasions beyond the sea. In the reign of Edward II. he likewise played a very prominent part. In 1310, his lordship was in the commission appointed by Parliament to draw up regulations for "the well governing of the kingdom and of the King's household," in consequence of the corrupt influence exercised at that period by Piers Gaveston; and in two years after, when that unhappy favourite fell into the hands of his enemies upon the surrender of Scarborough Castle, Lord Warwick violently seized upon his person, and, after a summary trial, caused him to be beheaded at Blacklow-hill, near Warwick. The Earl's hostility to Gaveston is said to have been much increased by learning that the favourite had nicknamed him "the Black Dog of Ardenne." His two sons, Thomas, Earl of Warwick, and John, Lord Beauchamp, both original Knights of the Garter, gained great renown at Cressy and Poictiers; the former as one of the principal commanders in the van of the English army, and the latter as standard bearer. The Earl's grandson, Richard, fifth Earl of Warwick, K.B., was distinguished in the battle-field and the tournament. A celebrated rencounter at Calais, between his lordship and three French knights, is thus recorded by Dugdale:—" The first of the French knights was called Sir Gerard Herbaumes, who styled himself 'Le Chevalier Rouge;' the second, a famous knight, named Sir Hugh Lanney, calling himself 'Le Chevalier Blanc;' and the third, a knight named Sir Collard Fines. Twelfth day, in Christmas, being appointed for the time that they should meet, in a land called 'the Park hedge of Gynes;' on which day the Earl came into the field with his face covered, a plume of ostrich feathers upon his helm, and his horse trapped with the Lord of Toney's arms (one of his ancestors), viz., *argent, a manch gules*, where, first encountering with the Chevalier Rouge, at the third course he unhorsed him, and so returned with closed vizor, unknown, to his pavilion, whence he sent that knight a good courser. The next day he came into the field with his vizor closed, a chaplet on his helm, and a plume of ostrich feathers aloft, his horse trapped with the arms of Hanslap, viz., *silver, two bars gules*, where he met with the Blanc knight, with whom he encountered, smote off his vizor thrice, broke his besagures and other harness, and returned victoriously to his pavilion with all his own habiliments safe, and as yet, not known to any, from whence he sent the Blanc knight a good courser. But the morrow after, viz., the last day of the justs, he came with his face open, and his helmet as the day before, save that the chaplet was rich with pearls and precious stones: and in his coat of arms, of *Guy* and *Beauchamp* quarterly: having the arms of *Toney* and *Hanslap* on his trappers, and said—' *That as he had, in his own person, performed the service the two days before, so, with God's grace he would the third.*' Whereupon, encountering with Sir Collard Fines, at every stroke he bore him backward to his horse; insomuch, as the Frenchman, saying, "that he himself was bound to his saddle;" he alighted, and presently got up again; but all being ended, he returned to his pavilion, sent to Sir Collard Fines a fair courser, feasted all the people, gave to those three knights great rewards, and so rode to Calais with great honor."

BRAY.—The name of the Sieur de Bray occurs on the Battle Abbey Roll; and although the authenticity of this celebrated record has in many instances been questioned, in this, the statement is confirmed by the fact of WILLIAM DE BRAY being one of the subscribing witnesses to the Charter of the year 1088, conferred by the Norman on the Abbey. No grant of lands appears, however, in Domesday Books to the Brays; but that the family supplied Sheriffs to Northamptonshire, Bedfordshire, and Bucks, between 1202 and 1273 is fully established. SIR RICHARD BRAY, the lineal descendant of the Norman knight, is said by some to have been of the Privy Council to Henry VI., but by others is called the King's Physician. By Margaret Sandes, his first wife, he had an only son, Sir John Bray, whose daughter and heiress, Margaret, wedded Sir William Sandys, afterwards Lord Sandys, of the Vine: and by Joan, his second wife, he had two other sons—I., SIR REGINALD BRAY, K.G., who was made a Knight Banneret at Bosworth, and who bore, in his arms, a thorn with a crown in the middle, in memory of his finding King Richard's crown in a bush, on the field of battle: and II., John Bray, Esq., who was buried in the chancel of Chelsea Church. This John had three sons—I, SIR EDMUND BRAY, Lord Bray, of Eaton Bray, co., Bedford, from whom derives Sarah, BARONESS BRAYE; II., SIR EDWARD BRAY, of Vachery Park, Cranley, Surrey, ancestor of the Brays of Shere, in that county, now represented by EDWARD BRAY, Esq., of Shere; and III., SIR REGINALD BRAY, progenitor of the Brays of Barrington, co. Gloucester.

BRACY.—A family of Brescy, derived from the Sieur de Bracy, of Battle Abbey, was connected with the county of Chester in very early times. The oldest document discovered relative to Wistanston in Cheshire, is a deed, without date, "of William Malbank, Baron of Nantwich, in which he gives notice that he has received of Robert de Bracy, his black nephew, ye homage and service of three Kts. fees—viz: for Wistanston, &c."

BELLET.—The Bellets were early seated in Norfolk, and became subsequently located in Cheshire by the marriage of John Bellet, Esq., *temp.* Henry VI., with Katherine, sister and heir of Ralph Moreton, of Great Moreton, in the Palatinate. Of this alliance, the lineal descendant, SIR JOHN BELLET, was created a Baronet in 1663.

BAUDEWIN.—The Sieur de Baudewin, whose name occurs on the Roll, became, after the battle of Hastings, Castellan of Montgomery, and from him that town acquired its Welsh appellation of *Tre Faldwin*, or town of Baldwin. There scarcely exists a doubt that this Norman Chief was patriarch of the ancient and respectable Shropshire family of Bawdewin, or Baldwyn, of which was THOMAS BALDWYN, Esq., of Diddlebury, who suffered imprisonment in the Tower of London, *temp.* Queen Elizabeth, and went through much suffering, as his epitaph, still remaining at Diddlebury, quaintly records :—

"Qui mare, qui ferrum, dura qui vincula turris
Quondam transivit."

His representative, after five generations, Richard Bawdewin, Esq., sold the Diddlebury estate to Capt. Frederick Cornewall, R.N., father of the late Bishop of Worcester. William Bawdewin, or Baldwin, second brother of "the prisoner," took up his abode at Elsich, in his native parish, and founded the branch seated there, and at Stoke Castle, which eventually acquired the lands of Aqualate, and is now represented in the male line by WILLIAM LACON CHILDE, Esq., of Kinlet, whose father changed his name from Baldwin to Childe.

BEAUMONT.—There existed at a remote period, a family of Beaumont in Normandy, and it was, probably, one of its cadets whose name was inscribed on the muster Roll at Battle. Certain it is that he could not have been the founder of the illustrious House of Beaumont, which, in two centuries after, appears so prominently conspicuous among the most potent barons of the realm, and which was established in this country by HENRY DE BEAUMONT, fourth son of Agnes de Beaumont, by her husband, Louis, second son of Charles, King of Jerusalem, and nephew of Louis IX. of France. From this great alliance sprang the various families of Beaumont; those of Stoughton Grange, Cole Orton, Grace-Dieu, and Barrow. Of the Grace-Dieu line was Francis Beaumont, the celebrated dramatic writer.

BLUNT.—RODOLPH, third Count of Guisnes in Picardy, had three sons, by his wife, Rosetta, daughter of the COUNT DE ST. POL, all of whom accompanied the NORMAN in his expedition against England, in 1066, and contributing to the triumph of their chief, shared amply in the spoils of conquest. One of the brothers returned to his native country; the other two adopted that which they had so gallantly helped to win, and abided there; of these, SIR WILLIAM LE BLOUNT, the younger, was a general of foot, at Hastings, and was rewarded by grants of seven lordships in Lincolnshire; his son was seated at Saxlingham, in Norfolk, and the great-granddaughter of that gentleman, sole heiress of her line, MARIA LE BLOUNT, marrying in the next century, Sir Stephen le Blount, the descendant and representative of her great-great-great-uncle, SIR ROBERT LE BLOUNT, united the families of the two brothers.

Sir Walter Blount, a descendant of this marriage, was much celebrated for his martial prowess in the warlike times of Edward III., Richard II., and Henry IV., and is immortalized by the muse of Shakespeare for his devotion, even unto death, to King Henry. Of the stock of Blount there were many flourishing branches: the Lords Blount of Belton, the Lords Mountjoy, the Blounts of Sodington, the Blounts of Orleton, the Blounts of Maple Durham, &c.

BEVILL.—The Bevills, sprung probably from the Norman of Hastings, were seated in Cornwall. Matilda dau. and co-heir of John Bevill, Esq.

of Gwarnock, married Sir Richard Granville, of Buckland, Marshal of Calais, *temp.* HENRY VIII., and had a son, Sir Richard Granville, a famous sea captain in the time of Elizabeth, whose grandson was the renowned SIR BEVILL GRANVILLE, one of the boldest and most successful of the Cavalier commanders. His last action was at Lansdown Hill, near Bath, and there he terminated his gallant career by an heroic death. His eldest son was created Earl of Bath, and his youngest, Bernard Granville, Esq., became Master of the Horse to Charles II. From the latter, derive the GRANVILLES of Calwich Abbey, co. Stafford.

BRETTE.—In the township of Davenham, Chesshire, was settled from a remote period the family of La Bret, which terminated in a direct line in Richard Breete of Davenham, early in the 16th century, who left two daughters his co-heirs; one married a son of the ancient family of Holfort, and the other wedded William Wyche of Alderley. The former had Davenham, and there her descendants continued to reside until the estate was sold by Allen Holford, Esq. to T. H. Ravencroft, Esq. Mr. A. Holford died in 1788, leaving daughters his co-heirs, one of whom, Anna Maria, married Joshua Walker, Esq., M.P.

Hamund la Bret witnessed the grant of Little Mereton to Gralam de Lostock, *temp.* Henry III.; and Richard le Brette de Daneham occurs among the contributors to the feast on the consecration of Vale Royal Abbey, A.D. 1336.

BARNIVALE.—About a century after the battle of Hastings, Sir Michael de Berneval, a scion of the family founded by the Norman knight, joined the English expedition fitted out against Ireland, and effected a descent upon Beerhaven, in the co. of Cork, previously to the landing of his chief, Earl Strongbow, in Leinster. Sir Michael is mentioned in the records of the Tower of London, as one of the leading captains in the enterprise; and in the reigns of Henry II. and Richard I. he was Lord, by tenure, of Beerhaven and Bantry. From this gallant and successful soldier derive the various families of Barnewall, seated in the sister kingdom; the senior lines being represented by Sir REGINALD BARNEWALL, Bart, of Crickstown Castle, and Thomas, Viscount TRIMLESTOWN.

BONETT.—The knight of this name who accompanied Duke William from Normandy, received for his services the lordship of Penclawdd, in Gower, which is corroborated by Fuller in his Church History, who quotes a MS. of Thomas Scriven, Esq., alias Fox, and the chronicle of John Brompton, in proof that, amongst others, "Bonet or Benet, was one of such persons, as after the battle were advanced to Seigneuries in this land, Glamorgan." A descendant of the Norman, Bonet, Robert Benet, who, *m.* Avis, dau. and heir of John Crompe, of Sanctuary, in Gower, and great grand-daughter, maternally, of

Caradoc ap Ynir ap Ivor, Lord of Dyfed, is supposed to have been the "Robert Benote" whose name appears amongst the Lances attendant on the Duke of Gloucester at Azincourt. Certain it is that he was direct ancestor of the BENNETS of LALESTON, CO. GLAMORGAN, now represented by JOHN BENNET, Esq., of that place. There is another family of the name, the BENNETS of Pyt House, Wilts, which can shew an unbroken descent from a period almost coeval with the reign of the Conqueror.

BARY.—Within a short period after the Conquest, William de Barri, a person of great power, the son, probably, of the Norman adventurer, *m.* Angharad, dau. of Nesta, dau. of Rhys ap Griffith, Prince of South Wales, and had four sons—1, Robert, styled "Barry-More," slain at Lismore in Waterford ; 2, Philip, ancestor of the several families of the name, so influential under the successive Lords Barry, the Viscounts Buttevant, and the Earl of Barrymore ; 3, Walter ; and 4, Gerald, the celebrated Geraldus Cambrensis. The Barrys were amongst the earliest Anglo-Norman settlers in Ireland, and have held large possessions in the county of Cork ever since the reign of Henry II. Many of their green acres have indeed fallen to the spoiler—and of the old Irish families, which may not similarly complain?—in the confiscations, political and religious, that so frequently and so ruthlessly visited the land of their adoption, from the accession of the house of Tudor to the extinction of the house of Stewart ; but still scions of the ancient stock exist on their hereditary estates, of which we may mention the Barrys of Lemlara, represented by GARRETT STANDISH BARRY, Esq., late M.P. for the county of Cork ; and the Barrys of Ballyclough, whose chief, JAMES BARRY, Esq , served as High Sheriff of that county in 1841. The name of Barry was ancient and noble in the Duchy of Normandy previous to the Conquest, and subsequently became preeminently distinguished in Wales and Ireland. In the latter country, the Barrys had immense possessions, and their chief seat, Castle Lyons, vied in splendour with the most celebrated mansions in the South of Ireland. Their earlier residences at Barryscourt and Buttevant, were also extensive and strong. A Lord Barry of his day, gave an entire barony (in England called a hundred) to an Earl of Desmond, as the marriage portion of his daughter. A younger son of one of the Lords Barrys, inheriting from his father the lordship of Rathcormac, built there the castle of Lisnegar, which continued to be the seat of his descendants in an uninterrupted line, until the latter part of the 18th century, when the last Barry of Lisnegar, being at feud with James Barry, of Ballyclough, his cousin and heir at law, made leases in perpetuity of some lands, sold most of the rest to Lord Cloncurry, Lord Riversdale, &c., and, in short, effected, in a manner, the ruin of his ancient house. The

Barrys of Ballyclough, spring from a second son of Barry of Lisnegar, and their present chief, James Barry, Esq., of Ballyclough, is the direct lineal representative of the Anglo-Norman Barry, who, with others, invaded Ireland in 1171. His property of Ballyclough, he inherits from his maternal ancestors, the Purdons.

BRYAN.—The great baronial house of Bryan became extinct, in the male line, at the death, in 1390, of Guy de Bryan, Baron Bryan, K.G., who served as standard bearer to Edward III. in the celebrated fight with the French at Calais. This potent noble left two grand-daughters, his co-heirs, viz., PHILIPPA, who m. 1st, John Devereux; and 2ndly, Sir Henry le Scrope, Knt.; but died *s.p.*; and ELIZABETH, wife of Sir Robert Lovell, Knt.

BODIN.—At a very early period, a family of Bodin, Beaudin, and Beadyn, or Beadon, for the name is thus variously written, enjoyed considerable property in Devon; but whether or not it derived from the Norman, whose name appears on the Roll, we have no means of ascertaining. From the Devonshire Beaudins, the Beadons, now of Gotton House, co. Somerset, claim descent.

BELLEW.—The founder of the Bellews, is stated, but on what authority we know not, to have been a marshal in the army of the Conqueror. Some of his descendants, of whom there were eighteen knights in a direct line of succession, settled in Ireland, at Bellewstown, in the county of Meath; and in the adjoining county of Louth, in the thirteenth century: of these we may enumerate the Baronets of Barmeath and Mount Bellow, and Sir Christopher Bellew, Knt., whose eldest son, Sir John, was created Baron Bellew of Duleek, a title that expired in 1772 with John, the fourth Lord, whose male representative is Captain FRANCIS JOHN BELLEW, H.C.S., great grandson of Patrick, son of Matthew Bellew, of Rogerstown, and nephew of John, the first lord. One branch of the family sprung from a common ancestor with the Irish Bellews, still remains in England, and is seated at Stockleigh Court, in the county of Devon.

BOTEVILLE.—The appearance of this name on the Abbey Roll seems sadly at variance with the statement of Matthew Paris, who records that the first of the Botevilles who came to England were two brothers, both of knightly rank, Geoffrey and Oliver Boteville, who brought a body of foreign auxiliaries from Poitou and Gascone, to assist King John against his rebellious barons. Sir Geoffrey, the elder brother, appears to have received a grant of the lands of William D'Albini, Earl of Arundel, at Shelton, in Shropshire, and was constituted Governor of Belvoir Castle. From his grandson, John Botevile, recorded among the knights of Shropshire, present at the siege of Caerlaverock Castle, derived John Botevile, who, from his residence in one of the Inns of Court, acquired the soubriquet of "John of th' Inne," and thence came the surname of Thynne, as now borne by John's descendant, the Marquess of Bath. The Botfeilds, of Hopton Court. co. Salop, and Norton Hall, co. Northampton, who formerly spelt their name Botevile, deduce their line from the old knightly race.

BRUTZ.—The family of Brutz, Brus or Bruce assumed its name from the Castle of La Brusce in Normandy, seventeen miles from Valognes, which was built by Robert de Brutz, or Brusce, a councillor to Duke Robert. His youngest son, Robert de Brutz, or in English, Brus, together with William, his son, followed the standard of their kinsman, the Conqueror, into England, where Robert is said to have died, very shortly after the battle at Hastings. William, his son, had the castle of Brember, in Sussex, and his descendants for several generations held rank as Barons of the realm. Adam, or Adelm de Brus, the second brother of William, came into England in 1050, attending Queen Emma; but, after her death, retired into Scotland. He joined his father and brother in the conquest of England, and for his services was rewarded with ninety-four lordships in Yorkshire. He died in 1079, and his son Robert is recorded in Domesday Book. He built the castle of Skelton, and founded the priory of Gisborough, in 1119; was at the battle of the Standard, in 1135; and died 1141, leaving issue—1, Adam, who succeeded to the lordship of Skelton, where his descendants continued to reside till Peter, the last lord, died, *s.p.* in 1271; and 2, Robert, who, marrying Agnes, dau. and heir of the Lord of Annandale, in Scotland, was grandfather of Robert de Bruce, Lord of Annandale, who *m.* Isabel, daughter and heiress of David, bro. and heir of William, King of Scotland; the great grandson of this marriage was ROBERT, "the Bruce of Bannockburn," the most illustrious monarch that ever swayed the Scottish sceptre.

SIR ROBERT DE BRUCE, grandson of Sir John de Bruce, second son of Robert, Lord of Annandale, competitor for the crown of Scotland, and grandfather of King Robert, had a charter of the castle and manor of Clackmannan in 1359, and eventually succeeded at the death of King David, as heir male of the Bruces. From him descend the MARQUESS of AYLESBURY, the EARL of ELGIN and KINCARDINE, MAJOR R. L. BRUCE DUNDAS, representative of BRUCE of AIRTH; Vice-Chancellor the Right Hon. Sir J. L. K. BRUCE, ROBERT BRUCE, Esq., Laird of Kennet, Sir MICHAEL BRUCE, Bart., Sir HENRY A. BRUCE, Bart.; BRUCE of KILRUTE, BRUCE of GLENGARRY HOUSE, BRUCE of GARTLET, BARBADOES, and RIPON; BRUCE of NEWTON and COWDEN, BRUCE of KINNAIRD, BRUCE of POWFOULIS, and the Viscount DE BRUCE in Paris.

BASTARD.—Robert Bastard appears in Domesday Book to have had large grants in the county of Devon, and thenceforward his descendants have remained seated in that shire, where they intermarried with the heiresses of Crispin and of Killiowe, in the county of Cornwall, and into the families of Fitz-Stephen, Besilles, Damarell, Gilbert, Reynell, Hele, and Bampfylde. Their seat, for many generations, was at Garston, near Kingsbridge, until, about the end of the seventeenth century, WILLIAM BASTARD, Esq., by marriage with the heiress of Pollexfen, acquired the estate of Kitley, which has since been the chief family residence.

CAMOIS.—The links between the Conqueror's companion in arms and the first recorded ancestor of the baronial house of Camoys have not been ascertained. We cannot ascend in the genealogy to a more remote period than that of the third HENRY, when we find RALPH DE CAMOIS restored to certain lands in Huntingdonshire, which had been seized upon by the crown in the preceding reign, owing to his participation in the rebellion of the barons. From him derived SIR THOMAS DE CAMOYS, of Broadwater, in Surrey, Knight Banneret, an eminent warrior of the times of Richard II., Henry IV., and Henry V., who commanded the left wing of the English army at Azincourt, and for his services on that occasion was honoured with the Garter. He had received summonses to Parliament as Baron Camoys, from the 7th Richard II. to the 8th Henry V. At the decease in minority of his lordship's grandson and heir, Hugh de Camoys, the barony of Camoys fell into abeyance between the last lord's sisters, Margaret, wife of Ralph Radmylde, Esq., of Sussex, and Aleanora, wife of Sir Roger Lewkenor, of Horsted Keynes, and so continued until 1839, when it was determined in favour of the senior co-heir, Thomas Stonor, Esq., of Stonor, co. Oxford, who now sits as Lord Camoys. The other co-heirs descended from Margaret Radmylde were Henry L'Estrange Styleman Le Strange, Esq., of Hunstanton, co. Norfolk, and Sir Jacob Astley, Bart., now Lord Hastings. Of Aleanora, Lady Lewkenor, the representatives (co-heirs to the barony of Camoys), were, Baroness Zouche, Katherine, wife of Captain G. R. Pechell, R.N., M.P., and Sophia, widow of the Chevalier Ferdinand de la Cainea.

CAMVILE.—Gerald de Camvile, the grandson probably of the Norman adventurer, was seated, *temp.* Stephen, at Lilburne Castle, co. Northampton, and in that reign granted two parts of the tithes of Charletin Camvile, in Somersetshire, to the monks of Bermondsey, in Surrey. His son, Richard de Camvile, founder of Combe Abbey, co. Warwick, appears to have been a person of great power during the whole of the reign of Henry II.; and in that of his successor, Richard Cœur de Lion, we find him one of the admirals in the expedition made into the Holy Land. The grandson of this feudal lord was Geoffrey de

Camvile, who received summonses to Parliament from 1295 to 1307.

COLVILLE.—Gilbert de Colavilla, or Colvile, accompanied Duke William from Normandy (where a town still bears the name), and was patriarch of the many eminent families of Colvile, both in England and Scotland; in the latter country ennobled as Barons of Culross. The representative of the Colviles of Newton, co. Norfolk, the chief English line, is now represented by CHARLES ROBERT COLVILE, Esq., of Duffield Hall and Lullington, co. Derby, only son of the late Sir Charles Henry Colvile.

CHAMBERLAINE.—John, Count de Tankerville, of Tankerville Castle, in Normandy, took part in the expedition against England, but returned after the battle of Hastings to his hereditary estates, leaving a son in the conquered country, who became chamberlain to Henry I., and whose son, Richard, assumed the surname of Chamberlain from his office. The chief line of his descendants were the Chamberlaynes of Sherborne, in Oxfordshire, from whom derived the celebrated Sir Thomas Chamberlayne, of Prince Thorpe and Presbury, a distinguished diplomatist in the reigns of Henry VIII., Mary, and Elizabeth. Of the existing families of the name, sprung from the Norman stock of Tankerville, we may mention the CHAMBERLAYNES of Maugersbury, co. Gloucester (now represented by J. CHAMBERLAYNE CHAMBERLAYNE, Esq.), and the CHAMBERLAYNES of Stoney Thorpe, co. Warwick.

CHAMBERNOUN.—The family of Chambernowne, originally Campo Arnulphi, yields in splendour of descent to few in the west of England, and was, at a period approximating very closely to the time of William of Normandy, seated at Clist Chambernon in Devon. Prince, in his quaint language, narrates that "there have been many eminent persons of this family, the history of whose ancestors and exploits, for the greatest part, is devoured by time, although their names occur in the chronicles of England, amongst those worthies who with their lives and fortunes were ready to serve their king and country." The eldest branch, that of Bees Ferrers, has merged in the noble family of Willoughby de Broke, and the next, which continued at Modbury, has long since expired. The Dartington line, however, still remains, represented, through an heiress, by the present HENRY CHAMPERNOWNE, Esq., of Dartington.

COMYN.—The career of this warrior terminated in three years after the Conquest. The earldom of Northumberland having become vacant by the decease of Earl Copsi, King William conferred it on ROBERT COMYN, the knight who had accompanied him from Normandy, but the nomination accorded so little with the wishes of the inhabitants, that they at first resolved to abandon entirely their dwellings; being prevented doing so, however, by the inclemency of the season, it was then determined, at all hazards, to put the new Earl to death. Of this evil design Comyn had intimation, through Egelwine, Bishop of Durham, but, disregarding the intelligence, he repaired to Durham, with seven hundred soldiers, and commenced a course of plunder and bloodshed, which rousing the inhabitants of the neighbourhood, the town was assaulted and carried by a multitude of country people, and the Earl and all his troops, to a man, put to death. This occurrence took place in 1069.

COLUMBER.—John de Columbers, a descendant of the Warrior of Hastings abandoning King Edward the First's standard in the French wars and joining the enemy, had all his lands seized.

CAUNCY.—The Sieur de Cauncy came from Cauncy, near Amiens. His descendant SIR HENRY CHAUNCY gained distinction as the historian of Hertfordshire. Many of the name and family are settled in that county.

CHOLMELEY.—Robert, son of Hugh, Baron of Malpas, is stated in Domesday Book to have held the Lordship of Calmundelei; and there is no doubt that the entry on the Battle Abbey Roll refers to him. He had no son, but was succeeded in his broad lands by his only dau. Lettice, the wife of Richard de Belward. The son or grandson of this alliance, William de Belward, Baron of Malpas, married Beatrix, dau. of Hugh Keveliok, fifth Earl of Chester, and had three sons—1, David de Malpas, ancestor of the Egertons; 2, Robert, who assumed the appellation of Cholmondeley, and was progenitor of the various families of the name, seated in Cheshire, Yorkshire, &c.; and 3, Peter, whose posterity, under the name of Clerk, was settled at Thornton, and became extinct *temp.* Edward III.

CHAMPNEY.—The Sieur de Champney is mentioned by Playfair as a younger son of the noble family of de Champnée in Normandy. From him descended the eminent Somersetshire house of Champneys of Orchardleigh, the last male representative of which was the late Sir Thomas S. Mostyn Champneys, Bart. A branch of this line fixed its residence at Ostenhanger, in Kent.

CHEINE.—The Conqueror's associate to whom this entry refers was Ralph Cheine or de Caineto. He received considerable grants of lands, and his descendants were seated, in high repute, at Sherland, in the Isle of Sheppey. One was the famous Sir John Cheney, K.G., created Baron Cheney by Henry VII. for his services at Bosworth: and another, that nobleman's nephew and heir, Sir Thomas Cheney, a person of great gallantry and note in the following reign. At the celebrated interview between Henry VIII. and Francis I., at Ardres, he was one of the challengers against all gentlemen who were to exercise feats of arms on horseback or on foot, for thirty days; and he became subsequently a knight of the garter, warden of the cinque ports, and treasurer of the king's household. Of the same family was the late General Robert Cheney, father of the present ROBERT HENRY CHENEY, Esq., of Monyash, co. Derby.

CURSON.—The ancestor of this noble family, who came over from Normandy, was, in all probability, Giraline de Curson, Lord of Locking, in Berkshire, whose name occurs amongst the most munificent benefactors to the Abbey of Abingdon. From him descended the Curzons of Croxhall, whose heiress, Mary Curzon, m. Edward Sackville, Earl of Dorset, K.G.; the Curzons of Kedleston, now represented by Lord Scarsdale; and the Curzons of Penn, whose chief is Earl Howe.

CLIFFORD.—This seems to be another interpolation of the monks, for the name of Clifford was not assumed until the reign of Henry II., when Walter, the second son of Richard Fitzponce, having obtained Clifford Castle in Herefordshire with his wife Margaret, dau. of Ralph de Toney, took thence his appellation. Though some doubt obscures this point in the Clifford genealogy, none exists with respect to their distinction and illustrious achievements in all historic transactions and in all martial enterprises, in court and in camp, from the stirring times of the Plantagenets to our own more peaceful days.

Henry, tenth Lord Clifford, and Baron Vesey, son and heir of the famed Lord Clifford, of the wars of the Roses—immortalized by Shakespeare's muse—succeeded to the hereditary honours of his illustrious house at the early age of seven, by the death of his father at the Battle of Towton. To protect him from the vengeance of the Yorkists, then in the ascendant, it was deemed necessary to disguise the young Lord in the mean habit of "a Shepherd's Boy," and to consign him to a herdsman's care. In that lowly condition he lived for twenty-five years, without any education, even so much as learning to write, lest it might lead to his discovery. On the accession, however, of Henry VII., he emerged from the Fells of Cumberland, with the manners and ideas of his humble associates. He was altogether illiterate, though far from deficient in natural understanding: but the consciousness of his own deficiencies depressed his spirit, and he determined on retiring to the solitude of Barden in Craven. There he found a retreat equally favourable to taste, to instruction, and to devotion. The narrow limits of his residence shew that he had learned to despise the pomp of greatness, and that a small train of servants would suffice him who had lived to the age of thirty a servant himself. His early habits and the want of those artificial measures of time which even shepherds at the present day possess, had given him a taste for observing the motions of the heavenly bodies; and he now resolved to seek amusement and instruction in the study of astronomy, under the guidance of the good and learned canons of Bolton, some of whom are said to have been well versed in what was then known of the science. In these peaceful employments, Clifford spent the whole reign of Henry VII., and the first year of the following. But in 1513, when almost sixty years old, the Shepherd Lord received a principal command in the army which fought at Flodden, and proved that the military genius of the family had neither been chilled in him by age nor extinguished by habits of peace. He survived the battle of of Flodden ten years, and died 23rd April, 1523, aged about seventy. He married first Anne, only daughter of Sir John St. John, of Bletshoe, cousin-german to Henry VII., and secondly Florence,* daughter of Henry Pudsey, Esq. By the latter, he had one

---

* The gradual advancement of this lady is remarkable; her father was an esquire, her first husband a knt., her second a baron, her last the grandson of a queen. She survived her father-in-law, who was slain at Towton, ninety-seven years; and having conversed with several of the principals in the war between the Houses, must, in the middle of the next century, if her memory remained, have been a living chronicle, fraught with information and entertainment.

Florence Pudsey was daughter of Henry Pudsey, Esq. of Bolton, grandson of Sir Ralph Pudsey, the faithful protector of King Henry VI., after the fatal issue of the battle of Hexham. The first husband she matched with was Sir Thomas Talbot of Bashall, the heir apparent of the knightly and historic family of Talbot of Bashall, the senior line of the illustrious house of Shrewsbury. He and his father, Sir Thomas Talbot of Bashall, adhering to the Yorkist party, co-operated with Sir James Harrington and Sir John Tempest in capturing Henry VI. Betrayed by a monk of Abingdon, the unhappy monarch was, in the month of June, 1465, taken by the Talbots as he sat at dinner at Waddington Hall, a seat of the Tempests, where he had found an asylum for several months. He escaped for a while, but was captured by the two Sir Thomas Talbots, near the Bungerly hipping stones, on the Ribble, across which he had fled for concealment in Clitheroe Wood, and he was by them conducted towards London. These events form the subject of one of Roby's Lancashire traditions. Warwick met Henry at Islington, and had the cruelty to subject his former sovereign to the indignity of having his legs bound with leather straps to the stirrups of his horse. In this degraded state, the King was led through Cheap and Cornhill to the Tower, where he remained for the next five years. Harrington received for his services lands belonging to Tunstall of Thurland, and the Talbots and Tempests received annuities out of Bolland and Tickle until they could be provided with lands. A tradition has been preserved that the luckless Prince predicted that there would be nine successive generations of his captors, the knights of Bashall, consisting alternately of a wise and a weak man, after which the name would be lost—a prediction, however,

daughter, Dorothy, wife of Sir Hugh Lowther, of Lowther, and by the former, three sons and four daughters. The eldest son Henry, eleventh Lord Clifford, lived upon bad terms with his father for several years, in conse- of his youthful dissipation; to supply the means for which he turned out- law, assembled a band of dissolute followers, harassed the religious houses, beat their tenants, and forced the inhabitants of whole villages to take sanctuary in their churches. He is said, however, to have been re- claimed in good time, and was created, 18th June, 1523, Earl of Cumber- land, besides being made a knight of the Garter. The barony of Clifford is now enjoyed by his Lordship's descendant, Sophia, Baroness de Clifford.

We cannot better conclude our reference to Lord Clifford, the Shep- herd, than by adding Sir Egerton Brydges' sonnet:

"To HENRY LORD CLIFFORD.

"I wish I could have heard thy long-tried lore,
Thou virtuous Lord of Skipton! thou could'st well,

From sage experience, that best teacher, tell
How far within the SHEPHERD's humble door,
Lives the sure happiness, that on the floor
Of gay baronial halls disdains to dwell,
Though deck'd with many a feast,—and many a spell
Of gorgeous rhyme, and echoing with the roar
Of pleasures, clamourous round the full-crown'd bowl!
Thou hadst (and who had doubted thee?) exprest
What empty baubles are the ermined stole,
Proud coronet, rich walls with tapestry drest,
And music lulling the sick frame to rest!—
Bliss only haunts the poor contented soul!"

The present representative is LORD CLIFFORD, of Chudleigh.

CORBETT.—Corbeau, a noble Nor- man, came over with the Conqueror, and, with his two sons, Robert and Roger, was employed by Roger de Montgomery, Earl of Shrewsbury and Arundel. Of the earl and his servants, Ordericus Vitalis says, "That the earl was a prudent and moderate man, a great lover of equity and of discreet and modest persons, and being freely assisted by the wisdom and courage of the said Corbeau, and his two sons, Roger and Robert, was as glorious amongst the greatest nobles as any of them

---

which the result has not verified, Sir Thomas Talbot the younger died 13 Henry VII., and, having no issue, was succeeded by his brother Edmund, an- cestor of the subsequent Talbots of Bas- hall, whose late representative and heir- general was Richard Hughes Lloyd, Esq. of Plymog, Gwerclas, and Bashall. Sir Thomas's widow wedded (as men-

tioned in the text), for her second hus- band, Henry Lord Clifford, representa- tive of the princely Cliffords. After his death, Florence took for her third hus- band Lord Richard Grey, younger son of Thomas Marquis of Dorset, and grandson of Margaret Widvile, Queen of Edward IV.

all, by keeping the Welsh in awe, and that whole province in peace." At the general survey, Roger, the elder son, held twenty-four lordships in Shropshire, and Robert, the younger, fourteen in the same county. Robert had a son, another Robert, Lord of Alcester, in Warwickshire, and two daughters:—Sibil, from whom the Herberts, Earls of Pembroke, and Finches, Earls of Winchelsea, descend, and Alice, from whom the Earls of Huntingdon. Roger, the elder son of the first Corbeau, left a son, William de Corbet, of Caus Castle and Wattlesborough, co. Salop, who was father of Sir Robert de Corbet, from a younger son of whom descended Peter Corbet, of Caus Castle, who was summoned to parliament, as a baron, *temp.* Edward I. The eldest son, Thomas Corbet, was great grandfather of Richard Corbet, Esq., who settled at Moreton Corbet, and his direct line continues still to reside there, being represented by Sir ANDREW VINCENT CORBET, Bart., of Moreton Corbet, co. Salop. The junior branches are the Corbets of Longnor, and Leighton, the Corbets of Elsham and Darnhall, the Corbets of Sundorne Castle, &c.

CHAUNDOS.—The name of the Norman who founded this great house, was Robert de Chandos, a successful soldier against the Welsh, and a munificent benefactor to the church. From him sprang the LORDS CHANDOS (whose eventual heiress, Alice Berkeley, granddaughter of Sir John Chandos, *m.* Thomas Bruges, ancestor by her of James Brydges, the princely Duke of Chandos,*) and

* Cannons, his Grace's splendid seat, stood on the road leading to Edgeware. The fronts were all of freestone, and the pillars of marble, as were also the steps of the great staircase. The gilding was executed by the famous Pargotti, and the hall painted by Paolucci. The apartments were most exquisitely finished and most richly furnished. The gardens, avenues, and offices were proportionably grand. At night there was a constant watch kept, who walked the rounds and proclaimed the hours. The duke also maintained a full band, and had divine service performed in a chapel that could hardly be surpassed in the beauty of its workmanship, by a choir of voices and instruments superior to that of any prince of Europe. For several years subsequent to 1718, Handel resided at Cannon's, as the duke's *Maestro di Capella*, and there produced the Oratorio of "Esther." But how fleeting is all earthly magnificence! At the decease of the duke, this princely edifice was disposed of piecemeal. The stone obelisks, with copper lamps, which formed the approach from the Edgeware-road, were purchased for the Earl of Tilney, for his new building at Wanstead, in Essex, which has since experienced the fate of the Cannons; the marble staircase was bought by the Earl of Chesterfield for his residence in May-fair. The ground and site whereon Cannon stood, became the property of an opulent tradesman, who built thereon a neat habitation, which still remains, after having passed into the hands of the well-known Colonel O'Kelly, of sporting celebrity.

the renowned Sir John Chandos, of Radborne, a pre-eminently distinguished warrior, and one of the original Knights of the Garter at the foundation of that illustrious order. On the memorable field of Cressy, this celebrated commander was entrusted by King Edward with the task of directing and defending the Prince of Wales; in the 30th Edward III. he fought at Poictiers; and in three years after, in consideration of his gallantry, obtained a grant from Prince Edward of two parts of the manor of Kirketon in Lincolnshire, to hold for life. In the same year, being retained by King Edward to serve him in the office of vice-chamberlain, he received £100 per annum out of the Exchequer, and shortly after, in recompense of "his great services in the wars and otherwise," had a grant to himself and his heirs for ever of the Barony of St. Saviour le Viscount, whereon he erected a castle. In 1364, the battle of Auray was fought against Charles of Blois, in which the famed Bertrand du Guesclin was made prisoner, and the victory there achieved is ascribed by all historians to the ability and prowess of Sir John Chandos, who had the chief command of the army of the Comte de Montfort. In the 41st Edward III. Sir John accompanied the expedition of the Black Prince into Spain, on behalf of Peter, King of Castille, and held a high command at the Battle of Nazar. He subsequently became constable of Aquitaine, and seneschal of Poictiers. The career of this gallant soldier, "the pride of English chivalry," soon after terminated, for, in 1369, he was slain in the wars of Gascoigne, in a skirmish at the bridge of Lussac, "to the great sorrow," adds Dugdale, "of both Kingdoms, whereof the King of France himself was so apprehensive, that he passionately said there was not any soldier living so able to make peace betwixt both crowns as he." He was buried at Mortemer, and his epitaph is recorded in "*Les Annales d' Aquitaine, par Bouchet*." He left no issue, whereupon his sisters became his co-heirs. Of those ladies, the third, Alianore Chandos, living 46th Edward III. *m*. first, Sir John Lawton, Knight, squire to her father, and constable, under that great warrior, of the town and castle of St. Saviour's; and secondly, Roger Collynge. By the former, Alianore left an only daughter and heir, Elizabeth Lawton, of Radborne, who *m*. Sir Peter de la Pole, M.P., for Derbyshire, 2nd Henry IV., and from this alliance lineally descends the present EDWARD SACHEVERELL CHANDOS-POLE, Esq., of Radborne.

CHAWORTH.—Patrick de Cadurcis, or Chaworth, whose name appears on the Battle Roll, was a native of Little Brittany, and after the victory of Hastings, appears to have been rewarded by grants of land in Gloucestershire. From him descended Thomas de Chaworth, who was summoned to parliament as a

Baron in 1299, and whose descendants continued for a long series of generations, seated in high repute in the counties of Nottingham and Derby. The eventual heiress was the "Mary Chaworth" of Lord Byron's poetry—

> "Herself the solitary scion left
> Of a time-honoured race."

This lady, who was only child of William Chaworth, Esq., of Annesley, *m.* in 1805, John Musters, Esq., of Colwick, and *d.* in 1832.

COURTENAY.—Loud are the vauntings of foreign genealogists on the surpassing brilliancy of Continental nobility; great the pretensions of Venice and of Spain; but, with all their boastings, no existing house in Europe can rival our own princely one of Courtenay. To use the eloquent words applied by Sir Walter Scott to the race of Douglas—" Men have seen it in the tree, but never in the sapling—have seen it in the stream, but never in the fountain." Scions of the emperors of the east, famous in war and in peace, they have ranked, from the earliest annals of the Plantagenets, among the chief barons of the realm; nor was it till after a strenuous dispute, that they yielded to the fief of Arundel the first place in the Parliament of England. In peace, the Courtenays resided in their numerous castles, appropriating their ample revenue to devotion and hospitality; and in war, they gallantly fulfilled the duties, and deserved the honours of chivalry. By sea and land, they fought under the standard of the Edwards and the Henrys. Three brothers shared the Spanish victory of the Black Prince; and an equal number, in the conflicts of the Roses, fell either in the field, or on the scaffold, for the cause of Lancaster. Their honours and estates were restored by Henry VII.; and a daughter of Edward IV. was not disgraced by the nuptial of a Courtenay: their son, who was created Marquess of Exeter, enjoyed the favour of his cousin Henry VIII.; and in the camp of the Cloth of Gold, he broke a lance against the French Monarch. But the favour of Henry was the prelude of disgrace; his disgrace was the signal of death; and of the victims of the jealous tyrant, the Marquess of Exeter is one of the most noble and guiltless. His son Edward lived a prisoner in the Tower, and died an exile at Padua; and the secret love of Queen Mary, whom he slighted, perhaps for the Princess Elizabeth, has shed a romantic colour on the story of this beautiful youth. The relics of his patrimony were conveyed into strangers' families; and in reference to these misfortunes, the chief of the Courtenays bore for centuries the plaintive motto of "Ubi lapsus! Quid feci?" This illustrious house is now represented by William Courtenay, EARL OF DEVON.

DANIEL.—There exists no doubt of the fact that the personage thus recorded on the Battle Roll, was the patriarch of the great Cheshire family of Daniel or De Anyers, of Daresbury and Over-Tabley, from which springs, through the female line, the Willis's, of Halsnead Park, co. Lancaster.

DE VAUS.—Three brothers, Hubert, Ranulph, and Robert, the sons of Harold de Vaux, Lord of Vaux in Normandy, accompanied William the Conqueror to England. From Hubert descended the Barons Vaux of Gillesland, which line terminated in an heiress, who carried the Barony of Gillesland to the family of Multon, from which it passed to that of Dacre. Ranulph, the second son, was ancestor to the Vaux's of Tryermayne, and maternally of Lord Brougham and Vaux. Robert, the third son, was the ancestor of the Lords of Harrowden.

DYVE OR DYNE.—An alteration in Domesday Book itself from de Dinâ to Divâ has led to the future confusion as to this name. Sir F. Palgrave, in his work on public records, describing Henry de Dyne, *temp.* Henry III., says, this name is sometimes written de Dive, and Dugdale uses the two indiscriminately. This family were actively engaged in the contests of the barons with Kings John and Henry III.; and at the final subjection of the latter, Windsor Castle and Forest were committed to Hugo de Dyne. They have held grants downwards from the conquest, one of them to Robertus de Dyna, by King Stephen, continued to them to the time of Cromwell's rebellion, when, in the hands of Sir Louis de Dyve, half-brother to Lord Digby, secretary of state to Charles I., it was confiscated by the parliament. They were thus of the baronial order in baronial days, and of the knightly, until that order went into disuse; Sir William Dyne being buried in Kent at the end of the 16th century, and Sir Lewis annihilated, as just stated.

The family, however, still surviving as holders of estates in Kent and Sussex, were allowed the hereditary arms during the rebellion in the name of Dyne or Dyve de Battersden, Kent, and had the same confirmed to them upon scrutiny after the restoration of the Sussex visitation, 1662. The name is now represented in Kent by F. BRADLEY DYNE, ESQ., of Gore Court, who still holds lands at Bethersden. The Sussex property passed to the Briscoes now of Coghurst, the grandfather of the present Musgrave Briscoe, Esq., having *m.* the dau. and heiress of Edward Dyne, Esq., of Coghurst, Sussex.

DISPENCERE.—Robert le Despencer, of the Conqueror's time derived his name from his office of steward to the king, and appears, from the numerous lordships he possessed, to have been a person of great eminence. His descendants—the two Despencers—the ill-fated favourites of the Second Edward, are too well known to require more than a mere mention here. The heir-general of the family is Mary Frances Elizabeth, BARONESS LE DESPENCER. Of the younger branches the chief are the Spencers of Wormleighton, represented by the Duke of Marlborough, and the Spencers of Althorp, by Earl Spencer.

DAUBENEY.—Amongst the most distinguished companions in arms of the Conqueror was Robert de Todeni, a nobleman of Normandy, upon whom the victorious monarch conferred, with numerous other grants, an estate in the county of Lincoln upon the borders of Leicestershire. Here De Todeni erected a stately castle, and from the fair view it commanded, gave it the designation of Belvoir Castle, and here he established his chief abode. He died in 1088, and was succeeded by his eldest son William, who assumed the surname of Albini or Aubeney, and acquired great renown at the celebrated Battle of Tenercheby, in Normandy, where, commanding the horse, he charged the enemy with so much spirit that he determined at once the fate of the day. From his eldest son WILLIAM derived the Lords of Belvoir, now represented, through a female, by the Duke of Rutland, and from his second son, RALPH, the Daubeneys, Barons Daubenay and Earls of Bridgewater, the Daubeneys of Gorwell, co. Dorset, and the Daubeneys of Bristol.

DARELL.—The descendants of this Norman knight established themselves over various counties, and for centuries flourished in all: the principal were those of Calehill and Scotney, in Kent; of Sesay, in Yorkshire; of Littlecote, in Wiltshire; of Pageham, in Sussex; of Trewornan, in Cornwall; of Lillingston Dayrell, Bucks; and of Shudy Camps, in Cambridgeshire. A curious trial is on record with reference to the Littlecote branch. Its chief was arraigned for the murder of an infant child, on the evidence of the midwife, who detailed, with most circumstantial minuteness, her journey, blindfolded, to a residence which she supposed to be the ancient manor-house of Littlecote, her presence at the birth of a male child, and her belief, founded on many circumstances she narrated, that the infant was burnt to death. On cross-examination, however, her evidence broke down, and Dayrell was acquitted, but the train of calamity which succeeded the trial may give rise to melancholy reflections, and was no doubt considered by the multitude to have been the effect of Divine visitation. In few words, the owner of Littlecote soon became involved in estate and deranged in mind, and is stated to have died a victim to despondency; and ruin and misery are said to have befallen the family that survived him.

DE LA POLE.—William de la Pole, Earl and Duke of Suffolk, the redoubted warrior of the martial times of Henry V. and Henry VI., was derived from the Norman De la Pole. From the same origin also sprang the De la Poles of Staffordshire, the parent stock of the POLES of Radborne, co. Derby, and the Poles, Barons Montagu, illustrious for having given birth to Cardinal Pole, Archbishop of Canterbury, the most eminent prelate of his age, one of the three presidents of the Council of Trent.

DELAWARE.—The family sprung from this noble Norman, became of great consideration, and had summons to parliament, *temp.* EDWARD I., EDWARD II., EDWARD III., and RICHARD II. Sir Roger de la Warr, the third Baron, son and successor of John la Warr, one of the commanders of Cressy, shared himself in the glory of Poictiers, and took a leading part in the captare of the French king. With reference to this exploit, it is recorded that much contention took place, as he defended himself with great valour; and the pressure upon him becoming great, such as knew him cried out, "Sir, surrender, or you are dead;" whereupon he yielded, according to Froissard, to Sir Dennis Morbeck, a knight of Artois, in the English service; but being forced from that captain, more than ten knights and esquires claimed the honour of taking the royal prisoner. Among these, the pretensions of Sir Roger la Warr, and Sir John Pelham (ancestor of the Pelhams, Dukes of Newcastle, and of the Lords Yarborough and Pelham) having been acknowledged the strongest, Lord de la Warre had, in commemoration of so valiant an exploit, the crampet, or chape, of the captive prince's sword; and Sir John Pelham had the buckle of a belt as a memento of the same achievement. His lordship continued for several years after Poictiers in the French wars, and acquired in every campaign an augmentation of renown. His only dau. Joanna, sister and heir of Thomas, 5th Lord Delawarr, *m.* Thomas, 3rd Lord West, and had a son and successor Reginald, Lord West, who was summoned to parliament as Lord Delawarr in 1427. This nobleman performed a pilgrimage to the Holy Land, 19th Henry VI., and died in 1451. It is related of his great grandson, Sir Thomas West, K.G., 9th Baron in the Rolls of Parliament, 2 EDWARD VI., that having no issue, he adopted his nephew, WILLIAM, son of his half-brother, Sir George West, and that the said William, impatient to inherit, had prepared poison to dispatch his uncle, which so highly incensed his lordship, that he complained to parliament, and William was in consequence disabled to succeed to his uncle's honours or estate, but had an allowance of £350 per annum. His lordship *d.* 1554, when the BARONIES OF DE LA WARE AND WEST fell into abeyance between the daus. and co-heirs of his brother, Sir Owen West, and finally amongst the descendants of MARY, the eventual sole heir. In a few years after, his disinherited nephew, WILLIAM WEST, having served in the English army at the siege of St. Quintin, in Picardy, was knighted at Hampton Court, 5th Feb. 1568, and created at the same time, *Lord de la Warre.* He had also, by act of parliament, in March following, a full restitution in blood, and was direct ancestor of the present noble family of DE LA WARR, with its derivative branch, the WESTS of ALSCOT PARK, co. Gloucester.

DESNY.— Isigny, a Bourg near Bayeux in Normandy was the patrimony of the Conqueror's companion in arms. Leland, in his Itinerary, p. 29, in enumerating the gentry of the Kesteven division of Lincolnshire, mentions " Disney, alias de Iseney; he dwelleth at Diseney, and of his name and line be gentlemen of Fraunce. Ailesham Priory by Thorney Courtoise was of the Diseney's foundation, and there divers of them buryed and likewise at Diseney." Lambert de Isney, of Norton D'Isney, co. Lincoln, is the first of the name mentioned in the public records. His descendants, of knightly degree, were seated for a long series of generations in Lincolnshire, representing the county in parliament, and allying with its best families. The present male representation vests in the family of DISNEY of the Hyde in Essex.

DABERNOUNE.—This family was early settled at and gave name to Stoke Dabernon in Surrey. Branches established themselves in Hampshire and Devonshire: in the last named county the heiress of Dabernon in Bradford, *m.* Dennis, *temp.* EDWARD I., and Joan the heiress of John Dabernon of Dunsland, *m.* John Batten, whose grandson by her, Humphrey Batten, of Dunsland, left an only dau. and heir, Philippa, who *m.* John Arscott, Esq., of Arscott, and was direst ancestor of the COHAMS, now of Dunsland

DAMRY.—The descendants of the Norman adventurer, the Damorys, were established in Somersetshire, 15 HEN. II. They bore for arms " Barry nebulèe of six arg and gu. a bend az."

DAUBROS, OR DEVEREUX.— Amongst the principal Normans who accompanied the Conqueror, and participated in the triumph and spoil of Hastings, was WALTER DE EVEREUX, of Rosmar, in Normandy, who obtained, with other considerable grants, the Lordships of Salisbury and Ambresbery, which (having devised his hereditary possessions and Earldoms to Walter, his eldest son,) he bequeathed to his younger son, Edward de Evereux, thenceforward designated of Salisbury. This potent noble, who possessed, at the General Survey, lordships in the counties of Dorset, Somerset, Surrey, Hants, Middlesex, Hereford, Buckingham, and Wilts, bore the royal Standard at the battle of Brennevill, and eminently distinguished himself. His only son, Walter de Evereux, founded the Monastery of Bradenstoke, wherein, in his old age, he became a canon. He was grandfather of William de Evereux, Earl of Salisbury, whose only dau. and heiress, ELA, was at her father's death, resident in Normandy. " This lady," says Dugdale, " being so great an inheritrix, one William Talbot, an Englishman, and an eminent soldier, took upon him the habit of a pilgrim, and went into Normandy, where, wandering up and down for the space of two months, at length he found her out. Likewise that he then changed his habit, and having entered the court where she resided, in the garb of a harper (being practised in mirth and jesting), he became well accepted. Moreover that, growing acquainted with her, after some time he conducted her to England, and presented her to King Richard, who, receiving her very courteously, gave her in marriage to WILLIAM, surnamed, Longespee (from the long sword which he usually wore), his brother, that is a natural son of King Henry II., by Fair Rosamond, and that thereupon, King Richard rendered unto him the Earldom of Rosmar, as her inheritance. Be this true or false, it is certain, however, that the great heiress of Devereux, Ela, espoused WILLIAM Longsword, *jure uxoris* Earl of Salisbury, the gallant soldier of the reign of King John, and one of the Crusaders at the disastrous battle of Damieta,* and left at her decease (she was then Abbess of Lacock) an eldest son, WILLIAM DE LONGESPEE, who made two pilgrimages to the Holy Land, and after a brilliant career, fell in 1250, in a great conflict with the Saracens, wherein the crescent triumphed. His grand-dau. and heiress, Margaret, commonly called Countess of Salisbury, *m.* Henry de Laci, Earl of Lincoln, and was mother of Alice, wife of Thomas, Earl of Lancaster. From Robert de Ewrus' youngest son Walter, Earl of Rosmar, the companion of the Conqueror, descended the DEVEREUX's Lord Ferrers of Chartley, and EARLS OF ESSEX, of whom the second possessor of the Earldom was ROBERT DEVEREUX, the ill-fated favourite of Queen Elizabeth—an able statesman, a gallant soldier, and one of the most accomplished noblemen of the period in which he lived. His Lordship is now represented by the Marquess Townshend, who, as heir-general, inherits the Barony of Ferrers of

---

* The Earl subsequently served in Gascony, whence, returning to England "there arose (we quote Dugdale) so great a tempest at sea, that, despairing of life, he threw his money and rich apparel overboard. But when all hopes were passed, they discerned a mighty taper of wax, burning bright at the prow of the ship, and a beautiful woman standing by it, who preserved it from wind and rain, so that it gave a clear and brilliant lustre. Upon sight of which heavenly vision, both himself and the mariners concluded of their future security; but every one there being ignorant what this vision might portend, except the Earl; he, however, attributed it to the benignity of the blessed Virgin, by reason, that upon the day when he was honoured with the girdle of knighthood, he brought a taper to her altar to be lighted every day at mass, when the canonical hours used to be sung, and to the intent, that, for this terrestrial light, he might enjoy that which was eternal."

Chartley. The present male head of the house of Devereux is Robert, Viscount Hereford.

DEUILE OR D'EIVILL.—The first mention we meet with regarding the descendants of this knight is in the reign of Henry I. when Nigel de Albini, being enfeoffed by the crown of the manor of Egmanton, Notts, conferred it upon ROBERT D'EIVILL, who appears to have been ancestor of JOHN D'EIVILL, Governor of York Castle, a potent Baron of the time of Henry III., and one of the most active against the Royal Cause. After the battle of Evesham, his Lordship returned not to his allegiance, but, joining Robert Lord Ferrers, made head again at Chesterfield, where, after the capture of Ferrers, he was unhorsed by Sir Gilbert Haunsard; he effected his escape, however, to the Isle of Harholme in Lincolnshire, and under the "Dictum of Kenilworth," eventually made his peace, and redeemed his lands by a pecuniary fine.

D'ABITOT.—At the time of the Conqueror's survey, Urso D'Abitot, the Sheriff of Worcestershire, held Holt Castle, and other large estates in Worcestershire, which had probably been conferred upon him for services at Hastings. His only dau. and heiress, Emelin, *m.* Walter Beauchamp, and left a son, William, ancestor of the Beauchamps of Holt. In some ancient records, Urso d'Abitot is called *Urso Vicecomes* and in other *Urso de Wirecestre*. About the year 1074, when Roger Earl of Hereford, and Ralph, Earl of Norfolk, conspired against King William, Urso united his forces with those of Wolstan, Bishop of Worcester, and Egetroyne, Abbot of Evesham, and did eminent service to the royal cause. He subsequently founded a hermitage at Little Malvern, in Worcestershire, afterwards converted into a cell of the Abbey of Westminster.

DAUNTRE OR DAUTRE.—In recording the foundation of Heryngham Priory by William Dawtree, the Monasticon thus speaks: "The latin word 'Ripa,' was in Norman writings generally meant for a river, without relation to 'Ripa' a bank. The Romans called it 'Haultrey.' There was an ancient family of knights, owners of much lands in these parts, and of fair possessions, even in the very bosom of the 'high stream' from which they took their name, and were called 'De Haultrey.'" "The ancient house" here alluded to was the stem of many important branches, the most flourishing of which was that planted in the county of Sussex, at Moor House in Petworth, not very far from Battle Abbey itself. It produced a series of knightly generations, which held the highest rank in their country, and intermarried with its noblest families. The last male representative, WILLIAM DAWTREY, Esq. of Moor House, Doddinghurst, died *s. p.* in 1758, having bequeathed his estates to (the son of his sister Sarah) his nephew, and heir, Richard Luther, Esq. of

Myles's, in Essex, who *m.* Charlotte, dau. of Dr. Hugh Chamberlen, the famous Court Physician, *temp.* Queen Anne, and died at Vicars Hill, Hants, in 1767, leaving a son, John, M.P. for Essex, who died *s. p.*, and two daughters, Charlotte, *m.* to Henry Fane, Esq., of Wormsley, brother of the Earl of Westmoreland, and Rebecca, who wedded John Taylor, Esq. of the Circus, Bath, and of Grosvenor Place, London.

Another branch, sprung from De Alta Ripa, is now represented by BENJAMIN DEALTRY, Esq. of Lofthouse-hall, co. York.

DE LA HILL.—The descendants of this Norman knight bore for armorial ensign, " Ar. two legs in pale gu."

DE LEE.—The Lees of Lee, and Darnhall, co. Chester, now represented by the Townshends of Hem and Trevallyn, and the Lees of Quarendon, Bucks, of whom was the gallant Sir Henry Lee, K.G., and the Lees of Ditchley, Earls of Lichfield, whose descendant Viscount Dillon now possesses the Ditchley estate, spring from the De Lee of Battle Abbey.

DRURY.—John de Drury, son and heir of the Norman adventurer, settled at Thurston, in Suffolk, and bore for arms " arg. on a chief vert, two mullets pierced or." His descendant NICHOLAS DRURY, of Thurston, living *temp.* Edward II., *m.* Joane, dau. and heir of Sir Simon Saxham, Knt., and by her had ROGER, NICHOLAS, and JOHN, from which three brothers derived the Drurys of Rougham, Saxham, Hawsted, Egerly, Riddlesworth, Besthorp, Everstone, &c. The founder of the Riddlesworth branch, was SIR DRUE DRURY, Gentleman Usher of the Privy Chamber to Queen Elizabeth, and one of the keepers of Queen Mary of Scotland. In the Drury family, there have been two Baronetcies—one conferred on Sir Drue Drury, of Riddlesworth, in 1627, and the second on Thomas Drury, Esq. of Overstone in 1739. The present male representative of this long descended line is GEORGE VANDEPUT DRURY, Esq. of Shotover House, co. Oxford, who is great grand-nephew of Richard Drury, Esq. of Colne, father of Sir Thomas Drury, Bart. of Overstone. Mr. Vandeput Drury represents also the noble and illustrious family of Schutz, and thus inherits a barony of the empire. The heiress of one branch of the Drury family, Jane, dau. of Henry Drury, Esq., of Ickworth, *m.* Thomas Hervey, Esq., and by this alliance her descendants, the Earls and Marquesses of Bristol, have become entitled to that splendid estate.

DUNSTERVILLE.—The heiress of the great house of de Dunstanville, *m.* about the middle of the 12th century, the representative of the Bassets of Cornwall, and conveyed to her husband the estate of Tehidy, which has since continued with her descendants, and is now enjoyed by Frances, BARONESS BASSETT, only child of Francis, late Lord de Dunstanville.

ESTRANGE.—Of this family (in Latin *Extraneus*) Dugdale says, "At a great just or tournament held at Castle Peverel, in the Peak of Derbyshire, where, amongst divers other persons of note, Owen, Prince of Wales, and a son of the King of the Scots were present; there were also two sons of the Duke of Brettaign, and the youngest of them being named Guy, was called Guy L'Estrange, from whom the several families of the L'Estranges do descend." How far this statement can be reconciled with the entry of the name on the Battle Abbey Roll, it is difficult to determine. GUY LE STRANGE was father of three sons, Guy, Hamon, and John, of whom the youngest, Lord of Ness, and Chesewardine, in Shropshire, obtained, 3 Henry III., the King's precept to the sheriff of that county for aid to rebuild part of his castle at Knockyn. He had four sons, John, Hamon, Robert, and Roger; of these, the second was ancestor of the Barons Strange, of Blackmere, and the eldest, of the Lords of Knockyn. The latter, John de Strange, Deputy Governor of Winchester Castle, and governor of the Castle of Montgomery, *m.* Joan, dau. of Roger de Somery by Nicola, his wife, sister and co-heir of Hugh de Albini, 4th Earl of Arundel, and *d.* in 1276, leaving a son and successor, John Lord Strange of Knockyn, distinguished in the wars of Gascony and Scotland. This potent noble married the heiress of D'Eiville, and had three sons. 1, JOHN, Lord Strange, whose last male heir, John, Lord Strange of Knockyn, left at his decease in 1477, by Jaquetta Wydeville, his wife, sister-in-law of King Edward IV., an only child Johanna, *m.* to Sir George Stanley, K.G. eldest son of Thomas, first Earl of Derby; 2, EUBOLO, husband of Alice, dau. and heir of Henry de Laci, Earl of Lincoln, in whose right he bore that title, he *d. s. p.*; and 3, HAMON, who was enfeoffed of HUNTSANTON co. Norfolk, 3 EDWARD II., by his brother John, Lord Strange of Knockyn, and founded the great and distinguished house of L'ESTRANGE of HUNSTANTON, now represented by HENRY L'ESTRANGE STYLEMAN LE STRANGE, Esq. of that place, who previously to the termination of the abeyances, was declared by the House of Lords to be one of the coheirs of the Barony of Camoys, and also of the Barony of Hastings. Referring to Hunstanton, Camden says: "It is the place where King Edmund resided nearly a whole year, endeavouring to get by heart David's Psalms, with Saxon language. The very book was religiously preserved by the monks of St. Edmundsbury till the dissolution of the monasteries. But neither is the place to be omitted upon this account, that it has been the seat of the famous family of L'Estrange, knights, ever since John, Baron le Strange of Knockyn, bestowed it upon his younger brother, Hamon, which was in the reign of Edward II." Of the Hunstanton line was the celebrated writer, Sir Roger

L'Estrange. A younger branch settled in Ireland, and is now represented by HENRY PEISLEY L'ESTRANGE, Esq., of Moystown, King's County.

DAKENY.—Baldwin de Akeny, grandfather of William Deken or Dakeny, Lord of Wrighton, in Norfolk, *temp.* Richard I., is presumed to have been the Norman knight whose name occurs in the Roll of Battle Abbey. William Dakeny's grandson, Sir Baldwin de Akeny, Knt., held a lordship in Holkham, *temp.* Henry III., and was Lord of Whittlesford in Cambridgeshire, A.D. 1266. He again was grandfather of Sir Roger Dakeny, Knt., who held one quarter of the town of Northwold in Norfolk, and increased his patrimony by marrying Johanna, the dau. and heir of Sir William Daubeny, by Isabella his wife, dau. and co-heir of Robert de Albini, Lord of Caynho. From this great proprietor the Manor of Dagenys in Norfolk derives its name. In the brief space to which we are confined, a passing reference is all that can be devoted to the knightly descendants of Sir Roger and the heiress of Daubeny. One of them, Sir John Dakeny, possessed, in the time of Edward III., a sixth of the barony of Caynho, and another, Sir Thomas de Akeny, Lord of Northwold, occurs as a gallant soldier in the Scottish wars of the first Edward. From his brother Humphrey Dakeny, the third in descent, Richard Delkyn or Daukyns of Hatten and Biggin Grange, co. Derby, returned amongst the gentry of that shire, A.D. 1433, was great grandfather of JOHN DALKIN of Biggin Grange, who *m.* Alice, dau. of John de la Pole, Esq. of Hartington, and had three sons—I. HUMPHREY of Chelmorden, grandfather of Sir Arthur Dakins, knighted at Theobalds in 1604. II. Arthur, of Linton and Hackness, co. York, general in the army, a justice of the peace, and M.P. for Scarboro', whose only dau. and heiress Margaret *m.* 1st, Walter Devereux, Esq., brother to the Earl of Essex, 2dly, Thomas, son of Sir Henry Sydney, K.G., and 3dly, Sir Thomas Posthumous Hoby, Knt. And III. Robert of Biggin Grange, living in 1543, father of John Dakyn, Esq. of Biggin Grange, returned among the gentry of Scarsdale Hundred in 1569. From him descended the DAKEYNES of Ashover and Bonsal, co. Derby, and the DAKEYNES of Stubbing Edge, in the same shire. Of the latter family was Frances, dau. and heiress of Arthur Dakeyne, Esq. of Stubbing Edge, and wife of Captain William Hopkinson, and from the same branch derived Mary Dakeyne, an heiress, who wedded Henry Gladwyn, Esq., and was mother of General Gladwyn. From the senior line, the Dakeynes of Bonsol, descended the late John Deakin or Dakeyne, Esq. of Bagthorpe-house, Notts, whose children are Henry C. Dakeyne, Esq., the Rev. John Osmond Dakeyne, rector of South Hykeham, Lincolnshire, and Frances, the wife of Frederick Polhill, Esq.,

M.P., of Howbury-hall, Beds. Of the same lineage also are Mr. James Dakeyne and Mr. Samuel Dakeyne of Sheffield, merchants.

DELABER.—The name of this Norman knight was SIR RICHARD DE LA BERE. A leading branch of his descendants became established at Southham, co. Gloucester, and bore, for arms, "az. a bend arg. cotised or, between six martlets of the last" From this family derives, in the female line, the present Rev. JOHN EDWARDS, of the Hayes, Prestbury, co. Gloucester.

ESTUTEVILLE.—The Conqueror's follower, Robert de Estoteville, became feudal lord of Cottingham in Yorkshire, and was succeeded therein by his son, also named Robert, who added to his inheritance the lordship of Schypwic, in the same county, by marriage with Eneburga, a Saxon heiress. The issue of the union was three sons—I. Robert, ancestor of the Lords of Cottingham, extinct in the male line *temp.* Henry III.; II. Osmund, progenitor of the Stutevilles of Dalham-hall, Suffolk, one of whom, Sir Martin Stuteville, served as sheriff of that county 10 James I.; and III. Patrick, who, receiving from his father the lands of Skipwith, assumed his name therefrom, and founded the great house of Skipwith of Skipwith, now represented by SIR GRAY SKIPWITH, Bart., of Prestwould, co. Leicester. The four daughters and co-heirs of Thomas Stuteville, Esq., a descendant of the Dalham line, married four brothers named Isaacson, of whom the eldest, the Rev. Stephen Isaacson, Rector of Freckenham, Suffolk, died in 1759, and is buried in the church of that parish.

ENGAINE.—Richard Engaine, Chief Engineer to the Conqueror, derived his name from his office, and founded the baronial House of Engaine. Joane, daughter and heiress of John D'Engaine, a descendant of the Norman warrior, married in 1381, Sir Baldwin St. George, Knt. of Hatley, M.P. for Cambridgeshire, and from this alliance derived the St. Georges, the distinguished Kings of Arms, as well as the noble family of St. George of Hatley St. George, and its flourishing branch, planted in Ireland, from which spring the St. Georges, of Wood Park, county Armagh, and Woodsgift, county Kilkenny.

FERRERS.—Henry de Ferrers, who accompanied Duke William to England, was son of Walchelin, a Norman knight, and assumed the surname he bore from Ferriers, a small town of Gastinois, celebrated for its iron mines. Hence, too, originated the "six horse shoes," the armorial ensigns of the House of Ferrers, allusive to the seigneurie's staple commodity, so essential to the soldier and cavalier in those rude times when war was esteemed the chief business of life, and the adroit management of the steed, even amongst the nobility, the first of accomplishments. The name of Henry de Ferrers occurs in Domesday Book, and from that record he appears to have had vast possessions, the greater part of which was parcelled out amongst his retainers; the Fitzherberts of Norbury and Swinnerton still hold the lands their ancestor thus obtained. Henry de Ferrers' chief seat was Tutbury Castle, in Staffordshire, but his most extensive territorial grants were in the adjoining county of Derby, whence his son Robert, the gallant commander of the Derbyshire men at the battle of the Standard, took the title of his Earldom. Of the illustrious race which sprung from this renowned soldier, we have space but to enumerate the different branches, and to add a passing word on their ultimate fate; the senior line lost the earldom of Derby, through the rebellion of Robert, the eighth earl, who was one of the most active of the discontented nobles arrayed against Henry III.: his son, John de Ferrers, inherited, however, the Castle of Chartley, in Staffordshire, and was summoned to parliament as a Baron. His representative, and the present inheritor of the Barony of Ferrers of Chartley, is George, Marquess Townshend. The Barony of Ferrers of Groby, conferred on William, grandson of William 7th Earl of Derby, merged in the higher honours of the Greys, Marquesses of Dorset and that of Ferrers of Wemme, acquired by Sir Robert Ferrers, younger son of the second Lord Ferrers, of Chartley, fell into abeyance in 1410, between Elizabeth Lady Greystock, and Mary, wife of Ralph Nevil, daus. and coheirs of the last Baron. Of the Ferrers', Lords of Egginton and Radbourne, the co-representatives are Richard Walmesley Lloyd, Esq,, (deriving his right through the Talbots of Bashall) and Edward Sacheverall Chandos-Pole, Esq., the lineal descendant of Sir John Chandos, by Margery Ferrers, his wife. The only male branch of the family still extant is that of Baddesley Clinton, co. Warwick, derived from Sir Henry Ferrers, second son of the Hon. Thomas Ferrers of Tamworth Castle, son of the fifth Baron of Groby. Its present representative is MARMION EDWARD FERRERS, Esq., of Baddesley Clinton, son and heir of the late Edward Ferrers, Esq., of that place, by the Lady Harriet, his wife, daughter of George, Marquis Townshend.

FOLIOT.—In the 12th year of Henry II., on the assessment of the aid for marrying the King's daughter, Robert Foliot certified that he had fifteen knights' fees which his ancestors had held from the Conquest, when his progenitor came from Normandy. His granddaughter and heiress, Margery Foliot, married Whyschard Ledet, son of Christian Ledet, Lady of Langtone, county Leicester, but her inheritance was litigated by the grandchildren of the male heir Robert Foliot. Of the offshoots of the parent stem was Jordan Foliot, summoned to parliament as a Baron, in 1295, and Gilbert Foliot, consecrated Bishop of Hereford, in 1149, and translated to tl see of London in 1161. Of h lordship, distinguished by his fidelity to Henry II., in the contest between that monarch and Thomas à Becket, Matthew Paris states the following circumstance:—As he lay in bed one night, after a conference with the King, a terrible and unknown voice sounded these words in his ears: "O Gilberte Foliot, dum revolvis tot et tot Deus est Astaroth." Which he taking to come from the devil, answered as boldly:—"Mentiris, dæmon, Deus meus est Deus Sabbaoth." Bishop Foliot was the author of an apology for Henry, against Becket, and he also wrote an invective against the proud prelate.

A branch of the Folliotts established itself in Ireland, and attained the honours of the peerage, its chief being created Baron Folliott, of Bally-Shannon. Henry, the last lord, left three sisters, his coheirs, of whom the Hon. Rebecca' Folliott *m.* Job Walker, Esq., of Ferney Hall, Shropshire, and was mother of Rebecca, the wife of Humphrey Sandford, Esq., of the Isle of Up-Rossall; and the Hon. Elizabeth Folliott, wedded first, Samuel Powell, Esq., of Stanedge, county Radnor, (ancestor, by her, of the present Henry Folliott Powell, Esq.,) and secondly, the Rev. Thomas Jones, of Combe, co. Flint.

The Rev. James Folliott, M.A., Pembroke College, Oxford, eldest son of the late William Harwood Folliott, Esq., of the city of Chester, and of Stapeley House, near Nantwich, descends, through a branch which migrated from Yorkshire to Londonderry, in 1640, from the old Baronial House.

FREVILE.—Alexander Baron de Frevile, the lineal descendant of the Norman, married Joane, granddau. and coheir of Sir Philip Marmion, and was great-grandfather of Sir Baldwin de Freville, who, in the 1st Richard II., claimed, as feudal Lord of Tamworth Castle, to be the King's champion on the day of his coronation; but the same was determined against him, [in favour of Sir John Dymoke, in right of the tenure of Scrivelsby. The last direct male heir, Baldwin de Freville, died, in minority 6th Henry V., when his great possessions were partitioned among the husbands of his sisters; thus Sir Thomas Ferrers had Tamworth Castle, Sir Richard Bingham, Middleton in Warwickshire, and Roger Aston, Newdigate, in Surrey.

FACUNBURGE.—The first of this name on record is Peter Falkeberge, son of Agnes de Arches, the pious foundress of the Nunnery of Nunkelling in Holderness. From him descended Walter de Fauconberg, of Rise, in Holderness, governor of Plympton Castle, Devon, who was summoned to attend the King, wherever he might be, to advise on the affairs of the realm, 22d Edward I., and shortly after had a seat in parliament as a Baron. By his marriage with Agnes Brus, he acquired the Castle of Skelton and other extensive lands, and had a son Walter, great grandfather of Sir Walter de Fauconberg, knight banneret, whose son, Sir Thomas de Fauconberg, sixth Baron, died in 1376, leaving an only daughter, Joan. This great heiress conveyed her inheritance in marriage to the youngest son of Ralph, 1st Earl of Westmoreland, the gallant Sir William Neville, who was summoned to parliament *jure uxoris*, as Baron Fauconberg, and subsequently achieving brilliant renown on the battle fields of France, and in the wars of the Roses, under the Yorkist Banner, was created by Edward IV., Earl of Kent, constituted Lord Admiral of England, and made a Knight of the Garter. At his decease in 1462, the Barony of Fauconberg fell into abeyance between his three daughters, Joane, married to Sir Edward Bedhowing, Knight ; Elizabeth, married to Sir Richard Strangewayes ; and Alice, married to John Conyers.

In an old inquisition, it was found that Henry de Fauconberge held the manor of Cukeney, Notts, by serjeanty, for shoeing the King's horses, when he came to Mansfield, which was formerly a place where our Kings were wont frequently to retire to, for the purpose of enjoying the chase.

FOLVILE. — The descendants of this knight were seated at Ashby, Bucks, and in the counties of Huntingdon and Chester. The arms they bore were "per fesse arg. and or, a cross moline or."

FITZ-ALEYN.—Alan, son of Flathald, obtained the Castle of Oswaldstre from the Conqueror, and is probably the soldier whose name is in the Roll of Battle. From him derived the illustrious House of Fitz-Alan, so distinguished under the title of Arundel.

FITZ-WILLIAM. — William Fitz-Godrick, father of the first Sir William Fitz-William, is stated to have been cousin in blood to Edward the Confessor, and to have been deputed upon an embassy by that monarch to William Duke of Normandy, at whose court he remained until he returned with the expedition in 1066, as Marshal of the invading army, and it is added that the Conqueror bestowed upon him a scarf from his own arm, for the gallantry he had displayed at Hastings. From this distinguished personage derives the present Earl Fitz-William.

FITZ-HERBERT.—Herbert, styled Count of Vermandois, accompanied Duke William from Normandy, and filled the office of Chamberlain to William Rufus. He received a grant of lands in Hampshire, and further increased his power by marriage with Emma, dau. of Stephen, Count of Blois. From him descended the Baronial family of Fitz-Herbert, a descendant of which, Adam Fitzherbert, Lord of Llanlowell, near Uske in Monmouthshire, married Christian, dau. and heir of Gwarin Dee, the black Lord of Llandilo, and was father of John Herbert ap Adam, Lord of Gwarindee, whose son William ap Jenkin, alias Herbert, resident at Perthyr, near Monmouth, *temp.* Edward III., had four sons, John, ancestor of the PROGERS' of Werndu; David, of the MORGANS of Arxton; Howell, of the JONES's of LLANARTH, and their derivative branch, the ennobled line of Ranelagh; and Thomas, of the chivalric House of Herbert, so celebrated under the title of Pembroke.

FITZ-WAREN.—This name seems to refer to the Fitz-Warines, who deduced from Guarine de Meez, a member of the House of Lorraine. Of this Guarine it is recorded that, having heard that William, a valiant knight, sister's son to Pain Peverell, Lord of Whittington, in Shropshire, had two daughters, one of whom, Mallet, had resolved to marry none but a knight of great prowess; and that her father had appointed a meeting of noble young men, at Peverel's Place, on the Peke, from which she was to select the most gallant, he came thither; when entering the lists with a son of the King of Scotland, and with a Baron of Burgundy, he vanquished them both, and won the fair prize, with the Lordship and Castle of Whittington. At this place he subsequently took up his abode and founded the Abbey of Adderbury. The last male representative, Fulke, seventh Baron Fitz-Warine, died in minority, in 1429, leaving his dau. ELIZABETH his heir. This lady became the wife of Richard Hankford, Esq., and the mother of Thomasine Hankford, who married Sir William Bourchier, Knt.

FITZ-JOHN.—Eustace Fitz-John (nephew and heir of Serlo de Burgh, the founder of Knaresburough Castle) was one of the most powerful of the Northern Barons, and stood high in favour with Henry I. His first wife Beatrice, only dau. and heiress of Yvo de Vesci, Lord of Alnwick, in Northumberland, brought him that extensive estate, and his second, Agnes, daughter and heir of William Fitz-Nigel, Constable of Chester, still further augmented his inheritance by the Barony of Halton. From Eustace's son, by his first marriage, William, sprang the great Baronial family of De Vesci: by his second alliance he was father of Richard Fitz-Eustace, Baron of Halton and Constable of Chester, ancestor of the Claverings, and the Eures.

FURNEAUX.—Within less than forty years after the conflict at Hastings, Henry I. granted the Manor of Fen Ottery, in Devon, to Allan de Furneaux, whose son Galfrid de Furneaux of that place served as Sheriff of Devon, in 1154, as did his son Sir Alan de Furneaux in 1199. From the Testa de Neville and other sources, the Manor of Fen Ottery can be traced in the possession of the same family down to John de Furneaux, *temp.* Henry V. A branch of this parent stem was established in Somersetshire, by Henry, brother of Sir Alan Furneaux, the Sheriff in 1199, and held the manors of Ashington, Kilve, &c. Three of its descendants, all bearing the Christian name of Matthew, occur on the list of Sheriffs of Devon: the last Sir Matthew dying in 1315, the year of his Shrievalty. Another offshoot fixed itself in Derbyshire, where Sir Robert de Furneaux, stated by Dugdale "to be a younger brother of the ancient family of Furneaux," was Lord of the Manor of Beighton, A.D. 1236. One line of this ancient house still exists, derived from Henry Furneaux of Paignton in Devon, whose eldest son, Matthew, was baptized in the church there in 1560. A scion of this branch settled at Buckfastleigh, and marrying in 1652 an heiress of the name of Kempe, became possessed of a freehold estate called Swilly, in the parish of Stoke Damerel, which has regularly descended to the present time, being now the property of James Furneaux, Esq., nephew of the Rev. Tobias Furneaux, of St. German's Parsonage, Devonport.

FURNIVAL.—The best authorities state that the first of this name, known in England, was Girard de Furnival, who came over from Normandy, *temp.* Richard I., and accompanied the crusade to the Holy Land. It is impossible to reconcile this fact with the entry on the Battle Roll. The male line of the Furnivals became extinct in 1383, at the decease of William, the fourth Baron, who left an only dau. and heiress Joan. This lady became the wife of Thomas Neville, brother of Ralph, first Earl of Westmoreland, and left a dau. and heir, Maud, who wedded Sir John Talbot, and thus entitled that renowned soldier to be summoned to parliament as "Baron Furnival." His Lordship's subsequent heroic achievements in France, won for him the Earldoms of Shrewsbury, Waterford, and Wexford, and thenceforward the Barony of Furnival merged for two centuries in the higher honours, until the demise of Gilbert, seventh Earl of Shrewsbury, in 1616. That nobleman left daughters only; the youngest of whom Alethea, wife of Thomas Howard, Earl of Arundel, eventually inherited the Barony of Furnival, and transmitted it to her descendants the Dukes of Norfolk, until by the decease *s. p.* of Edward, ninth Duke, in 1777, it fell into abeyance between his Grace's nieces, and still continues in the same state, the present coheirs being Lords Stourton and Petre.

GURNAY.—Hugo de Gournay, Lord of Gournay, in Normandy, who bore, for arms, pure *sable*, was one of the barons who commanded at the battle of Mortimer, against the French in 1054. Subsequently, coming over to England with Duke William, he participated in the victory of Hastings, and was rewarded with the manorial grants in Essex, which he held at the period of the General Survey. His son, Gerard de Gournay, Baron of Gournay, in Normandy, and Baron of Yarmouth in England, greatly increased his power and influence, by marrying the Conqueror's granddaughter, Editha, dau. of

William de Warren, Earl of Surrey. The issue of this brilliant alliance was one son and two daughters. Of the latter, the elder, Gundred, wife of Nigel de Albini, was progenitrix of the Mowbrays, Dukes of Norfolk, and the Albinis, feudal Lords of Camho; and the younger, who wedded Richard de Talbot, was ancestress of the Talbots of Bashall, co. York, and the Talbots, Earls of Shrewsbury. The son, Hugo de Gournay, Lord of Gournay, "educatus cum Henrico primo, et ab illo multum honoratus et dilectus," was great-grandfather of Julia de Gournay, the richly portioned bride of William Bardolph, Baron of Wirmgay. Thus ended the chief male line; two younger branches continued however to flourish. The one, which was the more distinguished, fixed its residence at Barew Gurney and Inglish Combe, in Somersetshire, as early as the Survey, and, retaining the name of Gournay, through two female descendants, added to its territory the estates of the Harpetrees and other considerable families, and became powerful feudal barons in the West of England. The most generally known of this line, were Sir Thomas de Gournas, one of the murderers of Edward II., and his son, Sir Matthew de Gournay, frequently mentioned by Froissart, who assisted at all the great battles of Edward III., and the Black Prince. The other younger branch of the Norman Gournays, held certain manors in Norfolk, as mesne lords, under the Barons of Gournay, the capital tenants, by whom they were subenfeoffed. Hence sprang the Gurneys of Harpley and West Barsham, from a younger son of which family descend the Gurneys of Norfolk, now represented by HUDSON GURNEY, Esq. of Keswick, F.R.S., and late Vice President of the Society of Antiquaries.

GEORGES.—Of the family planted by the Georges of Hastings, branches spread over the counties of Hertford, Dorset, Somerset, and Wilts. In the last named shires it was seated at Langford, and possessed so influential a position, that Sir Edward Georges, of Langford, obtained a baronetcy in 1612, and was afterwards raised to the peerage of Ireland, as Baron Georges, of Dundalk. That title is now extinct; but a male heir of the old family of Gorges still exists in the person of the present HAMILTON GORGES, Esq., of Kilbrew, co. Meath.

GERNOUN.—The descendants of this knight were a family of baronial rank, great possessions, and much personal distinction, the parent stem, it is stated, of the noble House of Cavendish.

GIFFARD.—When William of Normandy desired to invade England, many of his nobles held cautiously back from proffering aid, being wearied and impoverished by the continued struggles in which the Duke had been engaged since his father's death. But a few stanch adherents, amongst the foremost of whom were Walter de Gyffarde, Count of Longuéville, and Osborne, his brother, the sons of Osborne de Bolebec, coming nobly forward with offers of men, ships, &c., the laggards were thereby warmed to the undertaking, and 'the expedition was carried out. In the subsequent success of his chief, the Comte de Longuéville largely contributed, obtaining no less than one hundred and seven lordships in the conquered country, and was constituted Earl of the county of Buckingham. His brother Osborne had also his portion of the spoil, the fertile county of Gloucester being allotted as the locality of his reward. Here he held the extensive manors of Brimesfield, Rochemtune, Alderberrie, and Stoche; upon the first named of which he settled, and there subsequently a great castle was built, (*temp.* STEPHEN,) which continued to be the residence of the family until it was destroyed by the army of EDWARD II., in the Baronial war, *anno* 1322. From Osborne descended the BARONS GIFFARD of Brimsfield, and the GIFFARDS of Chillington, co. Stafford, now represented by THOMAS WILLIAM GIFFARD, Esq., of that place; Peter Giffard, Esq., the chief of the latter distinguished house, *temp.* Charles I., in his extended and chequered life, saw the entire downfall and the perfect restoration of his family. From the commencement of the great rebellion he appears to have taken an active and decided part in it, for at an early period we find his estates confiscated, and himself a prisoner. Chillington, recently receiving a royal guest in the person of Queen Elizabeth, became a royal garrison. The estates were sold by the Drury House Commissioners; and the members of the family, after fighting in the king's army as long as an army existed, were in prison, in banishment, or in concealment. When the second CHARLES made his ill-advised descent on England, in 1651, several of the Giffards joined him, and fought on the fatal field of Worcester. After his defeat, the king returned towards Kidderminster, and was advised by the Earl of Derby to seek a temporary retreat at Boscobel, where the Earl had been safely concealed for many days, during a hot pursuit, in an earlier part of the war. The king assenting to this proposition, moved with his few faithful followers in the direction of Kidderminster; but on Kinfare Heath, it being night, was terribly discomfited by the acknowledgment of his guide that he had lost his way. In this dilemma, a gentleman among his followers offered his services as guide; this was Charles Giffard, a nephew of Peter Giffard, of Chillington. Well and cleverly did he perform his task, guiding the royal fugitive safely and quickly to the spot where immediate security might be found. Peter Giffard survived the troublous period to which we refer, and after the Restoration, received (somewhat tardily) a royal grant of his estreated possessions. A few months after this, having survived his lady, and most of his contemporaries, he executed a deed, by which he surrendered all he possessed to his eldest son, reserving only for himself a small farm, the service of two retainers, and such maintenance (said the deed) "as was becoming to a gentleman of his quality." He did not long enjoy the calm this arrangement seemed to promise, but having seen his family reinstated in the wealth, influence, and honour which was their heritage, he died "full of days," 25th June, 1663.

GOWER.—This, we apprehend, is another monkish addition. All our antiquaries coincide in attaching a long and distinguished line of ancestors to the noble house of Gower, but they all assert for it an Anglo-Saxon origin. From a remote period its members acted a prominent part in public affairs, and so far back as the close of the 18th century, Sir John Gower was one of the persons of note summoned to be at Carlisle, with horse and arms, on the feast of the Nativity of St. John the Baptist, to march against the Scots. From him descends, in direct line, the present DUKE OF SUTHERLAND.

GRAUNT.—An error may possibly exist in the addition of the letter R to this name. Among the soldiers of the Conquest, few were more largely rewarded than Duke William's nephew, Gilbert de Gaunt, son of Baldwin, Earl of Flanders, and it is therefore very unlikely that his name should be altogether omitted in the Roll of Battle Abbey. Besides, we have no trace of any Norman knight bearing the designation of Graunt.

At the period of the general survey, we find Gilbert de Gant possessed of Manors in the counties of Berks, Oxford, York, Cambridge, Bucks, Huntingdon, Northampton, Rutland, Leicester, Warwick, Notts, and Lincoln, in all a hundred and seventy-three lordships, of which Folkingham was *caput baroniæ*. Like most of the great lords of his time, Gilbert disgorged a part of the spoil, thus acquired, to the Church, and amongst other acts of piety, restored Bardney Abbey, in Lincolnshire, which had been destroyed by the Pagan Danes, Inquar and Hubba. The son and successor of this renowned feudal chief was Walter de Gant, a distinguished commander at the Battle of the Standard, "where," says Dugdale, "by his eloquent speech and prudent conduct, the whole army received such encouragement, as that the Scots were utterly vanquished." He died 4 King Stephen, leaving a son, Gilbert de Gant, who became Earl of Lincoln *jure uxoris*.

GRANSON.—The first of the descendants of this Norman adventurer whom we find to have attained public eminence, was Sir Otho de Grandison, Secretary to King Edward I., and at one time Ambassador to Rome. He received summons to Parliament as a baron in 1299, but died without issue, when the title became extinct. From his brother, William, derived the subsequent Barons Grandison

GRAY.—Anschitel de Crey, or de

Grey, son of John, Lord of Croy, in Normandy, the Conqueror's companion in arms, held lands of the fee of William Fitz-Osborne, as recorded in Domesday Book. Of the ancient chivalric family of Grey, many branches had baronial summons to Parliament—the Greys of Codnor, the Greys of Wilton, the Greys of Ruthyn, the Greys of Rotherfield, the Greys of Groby, the Greys of Werke, &c. The Groby line has the proud distinction of having given birth to Lady Jane Grey, who was eldest daughter of Henry Grey, Marquis of Dorset, and Duke of Suffolk, by the Lady Frances Brandon, his wife, niece of King Henry VIII. The principal existing families of the name are those of Ruthyn, represented by the Marchioness of Hastings and Howick, whose chief is the present Earl Grey.

GRENDOUN.—This soldier of the Conquest received as his share of the spoil a fair lordship in Warwickshire, and thence assuming a surname, founded a knightly family, which obtained Baronial rank in the reign of Edward I., when Sir Ralph de Grendon had summons to Parliament, A.D. 1299. His only son, Robert, second lord, being of weak intellect, much litigation arose regarding the lordship of Grendon, with Sir Roger and Sir Philip Chetwynds (who were allied to the family by marriage), and endured for a considerable time. At length an agreement was entered into, under which the estate passed to the Chetwynds, by whose descendant, Sir George Chetwynd, Bart., it is now held.

GRENVILLE.—Richard, surnamed de Grenville, from one of his Lordships, was younger brother of the renowned conqueror of Glamorganshire, Robert Fitz-Hamon, and derived in direct descent from Rollo, the Dane. Accompanying his royal kinsman to England, he fought at Hastings, and participated in the spoils of victory. He inherited also the Norman honours of his house, and was Earl of Corbeil and Baron of Thorigny and Granville. From him sprang the Granvilles of Stow, in Cornwall, a race of men distinguished in each successive generation, but pre-eminently illustrious in the 16th and 17th centuries, when the achievements of the Granvilles illumine with their brilliancy the page of their country's annals. We can only glance in passing at the heroic death of the gallant Admiral Granville, the friend and relative of Raleigh, and exclaim with John Evelyn, than this, "what have we more? What can be greater?" His two grandsons, however, acted so conspicuous a part in the Civil War, that we cannot omit a slight reference to their exploits. The elder, the famed Sir Bevil Granville, one of the boldest and most successful of the Cavalier leaders, joined the Royal Standard on the first outbreak of the rebellion; and marching into Cornwall, rescued that whole county from the Parliament, attacked the partisans of the Commons, who had risen in great numbers in the west, and routed them at Bodmin, Launceston, and Stratton. His last and most brilliant action was at Lansdown Hill, near Bath, where he fell in the arms of victory, on the 5th July, 1643. "On the king's part," says Clarendon in detailing this engagement, "there were more officers and gentlemen of quality slain than common men, and more hurt than slain. That which would have clouded any victory and made the loss of others less spoken of was the death of Sir Bevil Granville."

The younger brother of this gallant soldier, Sir Richd. Granville, was also a Cavalier commander of great celebrity, who advanced the Royal cause, in an especial degree, by his consummate skill and chivalrous bravery. He eventually fixed his residence in France, and dying at Ghent, was interred in the English church, where this simple inscription marks the sacred spot: "Sir Richard Granville, the king's general in the west." In more recent times, the name of Granville again became distinguished in the person of George Granville, Lord Lansdowne, a poet of considerable reputation. The present representative of this illustrious race is COURT GRANVILLE, Esq., of Calwich Abbey, co. Stafford.

GURDON.—The Seigneurie of Gourdon near Cahors, on the borders of Perigord, was the patrimony of this Norman adventurer. His descendant, Sir Adam de Gurdon, Knt., living *temp.* Henry III., was in that monarch's reign Bailiff of Alton: but joining the Mountford faction, he suffered outlawry, which was not removed until the following reign, when Sir Adam received the custody of the forest of Wolmer. From this celebrated knight, whose lands at Selborne, Hants, known still as Gurdon manor, belong to Magdalen College, Oxford, spring the GURDONS of ASSINGTON, co. Suffolk, and the GURDONS of LETTON, co. Norfolk. The former estate was purchased from Sir Miles Corbet, by Robert Gurdon, Esq., in the 16th century, and the latter acquired by his son, John Gurdon, Esq., in marriage with Amy, dau. and heir of Wm. Brampton, Esq.

GUINES.—In the reign of King John we find Ernold Count of Ghisnes in France possessed of twelve knights' fees in England. His son and heir was Baldwin Ghisnes and the next on record, Robert de Ghisnes, living A.D. 1248, is styled uncle to Arnulph, Earl of Ghisnes. The name does not again occur until 1 Edward I., when we meet with mention of Ingelram de Ghisnes, otherwise de Cursi, a noble Baron of France, whose successor, also named Ingelram, a distinguished commander in the Scottish wars, was summoned to Parliament as a baron. The grandson of this nobleman, Ingelram de Ghisnes or de Courcy, allying himself to the Royal House of Plantagenet by his marriage with the Lady Isabella, daughter of Edward III., received a grant of the Earldom of Bedford, with the ribbon of the Garter.

HAUNSARD.—The descendants of

this Norman established themselves in the counties of York, Lincoln, Lancaster, Sussex, &c., and bore for arms " Gu. three mullets or." A scion of the Yorkshire branch, settled in Ireland, *temp.* JAMES II., was represented by the late RICHARD MASSEY HANSARD, Esq., of Miskin House, Glamorganshire.

HASTINGS.—Robert, Steward to William of Normandy, accompanied the expedition to England, and was rewarded with the Lordship of Fillongley, co. Warwick. He received also the appointment of Portgrave of Hastings, and thence arose a surname, which his illustrious descendants rendered renowned in the cabinet and in the field. Robert's successor, Walter de Hastings, became steward to Henry I., as owner of the manor of Ashills, co. Norfolk, which he held on condition of taking charge of the *naperie* (table linen) at the Coronation. His descendant, Henry de Hastings, Baron Hastings, married Ada, daughter of David, Earl of Huntingdon, and was father of the bold defender of Kenilworth Castle, Henry, Lord Hastings, whose grandson, John Hastings, seneschal of Aquitaine, was one of the aspirants to the Scottish throne, A.D. 1290, in right of his great grandmother, Ada, who was niece to William the Lion. This potent noble wedded for his first wife, Isabel, sister and co-heir of Aymer de Valence, Earl of Pembroke, and had by her a son John, ancestor of the Earls of Pembroke, whose last representative, John Hastings, third Earl, was accidentally slain in a tournament, by Sir John St. John, at Woodstock, in 1389. The superstition of the period attributed the untimely fate of the youthful Earl to a divine judgment upon the family, in regard that Aymer de Valence, Earl of Pembroke his ancestor, was one of those who passed sentence of death upon Thomas Plantagenet, Earl of Lancaster, at Pontefract: for, it was observed, that subsequently to that judgment, not one of the Earls of Pembroke saw his father, nor any father of them took delight in seeing his children.

From the second marriage of John de Hastings, the competitor for the throne of Scotland, derived the Lord Hastings of Gressing Hall. One great branch of the family still exists, that represented in the male line, by the EARL OF HUNTINGDON. It springs from Thomas, a younger son of William de Hastings, steward to Henry II., grandson of Walter de Hastings, Lord of Fillingley, steward to Henry I.; and was first ennobled in the person of the celebrated Sir William Hastings, created Baron Hastings of Ashby-de-la-Zouch, by King Edward IV., in 1461. His lordship, who was one of the most powerful persons in the kingdom, erected at Ashby, a magnificent castle, which continued to be for two hundred years the residence of his descendants, and was afterwards remarkable as the temporary prison of Mary, Queen of Scots. He fell a victim, eventually, to the Protector Gloucester, and was be-

beheaded in the Tower, A.D. 1483. Of his Lordship, Fuller says—" The reder needeth not my dim candle to direct him to this illustrious person, whom King Edward IV., or rather Edward Plantagenet (because more in human than in his royal capacity) so delighted in, that he made him his Lord Chamberlain, Baron Hastings of Ashby-de-la-Zouch, &c." The first Earl of Huntingdon was this nobleman's grandson, George, who attended Henry VIII. to Therouenne and Tournay, and was rewarded with an earl's coronet. His son, the second Earl, formed a brilliant alliance, marrying Katherine, daughter and co-heir of Henry Pole Lord Montagu, and granddaughter of Margaret, Countess of Salisbury, daughter and sole heir of George Plantagenet, Duke of Clarence, brother of Edward IV. By this high-born lady he had six sons and five daughters: of the youngest of the latter, the beautiful Lady Mary Hastings, the following circumstance is related:—" John Vassilivich, Great Duke and Emperor of Russia, having a desire to marry an English lady, was told of the Lady Mary Hastings, who being of the blood royal, he began to affect, whereupon making his desires known to Queen Elizabeth, who did well approve thereof, he sent over Theodore Pissemskoie, a nobleman of great account, his ambassador, who, in the name of his master, offered great advantage to the Queen in the event of the marriage. The Queen hereupon caused the lady to be attended with divers ladies and young noblemen, that so the ambassador might have a sight of her, which was accomplished in York House Garden, near Charing Cross. There, was the envoy brought into her presence, and casting down his countenance, fell prostrate before her, then rising back with his face still towards her, (the lady with the rest admiring at his strange salutation), he said, by his interpreter, 'it sufficed him to behold the angelic presence of her who, he hoped, would be his master's spouse and empress!'" The alliance did not, however, take place, and the lady died unmarried.

HUSEE.—The visitation of Dorset, A.D. 1623, as well as a manuscript in ancient French said to have been found in the Abbey of Glastonbury at its dissolution, records that HUBERT HUSEE, a Norman noble, having married the Countess Helen, dau. of Richard 5th Duke of Normandy, accompanied the Conqueror to England, and had a grant of the office of High Constable, with considerable possessions. Certain it is that the family of Hussey appears among the great landed proprietors at a very early period, and soon attained a distinguished position in various parts of the Kingdom. In the reign of the fourth Edward, Sir William Hussey, an eminent lawyer, held the dignified office of Lord Chief Justice of the King's Bench, and his son Sir John Hussey was elevated to the peerage by Henry VIII., as Baron Hussey of Sleford, in 1534. A younger branch, the HUSSEYS of HONINGTON, co. Lincoln, distinguished for their devotion to the Royal cause, obtained a Baronetcy from James I. in 1611, but their male line expired in 1734. Charlotte, sister and heiress of Sir Edward Hussey, the last Baronet, m. Thomas Pochin, Esq. of Barkby, and was mother of Charlotte Pochin, wife of CHARLES JAMES PACKE, Esq., of Prestwold-hall, co. Leicester. So far back as the time of Henry II., a scion of the house, Sir Hugh Hussey, went to Ireland, wedded the sister of Theobald Fitz-Walter, the first Butler of that kingdom, and died seised of large possessions in the county of Meath from the grant of Hugh de Lacie. He was ancestor of the HUSSEYS, BARONS of GALTRIM, of whom the Husseys of Westown, co. Dublin, are a derivative branch.

In England some descendants of the Norman Husèe still exist, among whom we may mention the HUSSEYS of LYME and MARNHULL, co. DORSET, and the HUSSEYS of SCOTNEY CASTLE, KENT.

HERCY.—In the reign of Henry III., Malveysin de Hercy, doubtless a descendant of the Hercy, of the Battle Roll, was Constable of Tykhill. He acquired by his marriage with Theophania, dau. and coheir of Gilbert de Arches, the estate of Grove, Notts, a d became ancestor of the Hercys of that place; and also of the Hercys of Cruchfield, Berks, now represented by JOHN HERCY, Esq. of Cruchfield.

HERIOUN.—From this adventurer sp ang the warlike race of Heron, so celebrated in Border feud and Border minstrelsy. In 1100, they possessed by grant from Henry I., the Barony of Heron in Northumberland, and in 1166, exactly a century after their Norman ancestor set foot in England, Jordan Hairun is named in the *Liber niger Scuccarii*, amongst the knights then enjoying great estates in the north. In the reign of Henry III., the marriage of William Heriun, Governor of Bamborough Castle, with the daughter and heir of Odonel de Ford, transplanted the family to the lands of her inheritance and there—at Ford Castle—they continued in high repute for several generations, William Heron of Ford being summoned to parliament as a Baron in 1371. In the contests between Percy and Douglas, the Herons were arrayed under the banner of the former, and at the memorable Battle of Otterburn, their chief, Sir William Heron, fought with distinguished bravery. The Ballad of Chevy Chase erroneously ranks him among the slain:

Thear was slayne with the Lord Perse,
Sir John of Agerstone,
Sir Roger the Hinde Hartly,
Sir William the bolde Hearone.

The history of the Herons and their achievements in all their various lines, would fill a volume: here we must content ourselves with enumerating some of the more distinguished branches: next in importance to that of Ford, were the Herons of Prudhoe, the Herons of Chipchase, the Herons of Cressy, and the Herons of Newark-upon-Trent.

HARECOURT.— Errand de Har

court (descended from Bernard the Dane, to whom Rollo of Normandy granted, A.D. 876, the Lordship of Harcourt in that Duchy), commanded the Archers of Val de Ruel in the Conqueror's army, but returned to his hereditary possessions immediately after William's coronation. His next brother Robert, however, who had also accompanied the expedition to England, remained in the conquered country. His son, William de Harcourt, a gallant adherent of Henry I., against Robert Curthose, commanded the troops which defeated the Earl of Mellent in 1123, and received in recompense a great addition of territory in England. Of his three sons, the eldest, ROBERT, Baron of Harcourt, Elbœuf, &c., was ancestor of the Viscounts of Chatelleraut, the Comtes d'Harcourt, the Marquises and Dukes of Harcourt, in France; and the second, Ivo, who inherited all his father's English possessions, became the founder of the noble House of HARCOURT in this country, of which was the famous lawyer, SIMON, Lord HARCOURT, Lord Chancellor *temp.* Queen Anne. The present male representative of the English Harcourts is GEORGE SIMON HARCOURT, Esq. of Ankerwycke, co. Bucks, who descends from Philip Harcourt, Esq., brother of the Lord Chancellor Harcourt.

HOUELL OR HOVELL.—The descendants of the Norman Houell were seated in the counties of Norfolk and Suffolk, at Hillington in the former and at Ashfield in the latter, bearing for arms, "sa. a cross. or." One of them, Richard Hovell, squire of the body to Henry V., was ancestor of the family of Hovell, which adopted the surname of Smith, and the coheiress of which, Elizabeth, dau. of Robert Smith, *alias* Hovell, Esq., *m.* in 1730, the Rev. Thomas Thurlow, Rector of Ashfield, co. Suffolk, and had three sons, EDWARD Lord Thurlow, Lord Chancellor, Thomas, Bishop of Durham (whose son Edward, late Lord Thurlow, took the additional surname of Hovell), and John, Alderman of Norwich.

HAKET.—The Hackets of Niton, in the Isle of Wight, were the descendants of the Haket of the Battle Abbey Roll. The eventual heiress, Agnes, dau. of John Hackett, Esq. of Niton, *m.* John Lye, Esq., of Dorsetshire, and was mother of Anne Lye, wife of Sir James Worsley, constable of Carisbrook Castle. Dominus Paganus de Haket, who also derived his descent from the soldier of Hastings, accompanied Henry II. to Ireland, and acquired broad lands and seignories there; and his descendants, generation after generation, were parliamentary Barons, and potent Magnates in the sister kingdom. They are now represented by MICHAEL HACKETT, Esq. of Brooklawn, co. Dublin.

HAMOUND.—Among the many of his own kin, who accompanied the Duke of Normandy on his invasion of England, were two brothers, sons or grandsons of Hamon Dentatus,—Robert Fitz-Hamon, the renowned

Conqueror of Glamorganshire; and Haimon, called in the Domesday Survey, "Dapifer," from his having received the office of Lord Steward for the King. The latter *d.* issueless; and the former left four daughters only, three of whom devoted themselves to conventual lives, and the fourth, Mabel, *m.* Robert Fitzroy, Earl of Gloucester. Haimon Dentatus appears to have had at least two other sons, RICHARD of Granville and Corbeil, ancestor of the Granville family, illustrious in the ranks of the peers and landed proprietors; and CREUQUER, as he is styled in the Battle Abbey Roll, who inherited the Barony of Chatham from Robert Fitz-Hamon and many of the Kentish estates of Hamon Dapifer. Creuquer, or Crevecœur, had his manors erected into a lordship, called by distinction "Baronia de Crévequer," and from Chatham being its head, his descendants generally wrote themselves DOMINI DE CETHAM. We find these honours, in the reign of Richard I., in possession of Haimon de Crévequer, who *d.* in 1203, leaving Robert Haimon his heir. Haimon joined in the confederacy of the Barons under Simon de Montfort against Henry III., and was among those who in consequence lost their estates. From him lineally descended Ralph Heyman or Hayman, of Sellinge, co. Kent, ancestor of the Heymans of Somerfield, extinct Baronets, and Roger Hayman, who, to avoid religious persecutions in Queen Mary's reign, fled into Devonshire, where he established a line represented now both in Somersetshire and Ireland. The present chief of the Irish portion of the family is MATTHEW HAYMAN, Esq., of South Abbey, Youghal, a magistrate for the county of Cork.

KARRE.—Two brothers, Ralph and John, descended from the Norman Karre, passed from England into Scotland sometime in the 13th century, and laid the foundation of those two illustrious Houses, KER of FERNIHURST, now represented by the Marquess of Lothian, and KER of CESFORD, whose chief is the DUKE OF ROXBURGHE.

KIRIELL.—Robert, Duke of Normandy, the Conqueror's father, in order to keep in check the people of the Pays de Dol, built in the year 1030 a castle at Cazel or Cheruel upon the Coesnon, a river which then divided the provinces of Normandy and Brittany. This place gave name to a family, which became highly distinguished in succeeding generations, and of which was the Norman knight, Kiriel, who appears on the Battle Abbey Roll. Among the more celebrated personages of the name, we may mention Hue Kyriel, Admiral of the French, and Nicholas Kiriel, Admiral of the English Fleet, in the 14th century; Yvon Cheruel, the brother in arms of Bertrand du Guesclin, and Sir Thomas Kyriel, K.G., a gallant military Commander, and a devoted adherent of the house of York, who was beheaded by Queen Margaret, after the second battle of St. Albans. The only family of eminence bearing a similar name and similar arms now existing in this country, is that of KYRLE, of Much Marcle, co. Hereford, represented by WILLIAM MONEY-KYRLE, Esq. of Hom House, one of whose collateral ancestors, JOHN KYRLE, has acquired from Pope, as the MAN OF ROSS, a claim to immortality more deserving of the world's esteem, than could be derived from all the honours of war. The family of Stansfeld, of Stansfeld, and of the Island of Jersey, deriving from Wyon Maryon, of a noble house in Brittany, to whom the extensive township in the West Riding of Yorkshire, whence he adopted his surname, was granted by the Conqueror, claims a common origin with the Kyriels and Kyrles, from the Kiriell of the Battle Abbey Roll. Claude Marion, Seigneur de Kerhouel, had confirmation, in 1669, of the noble descent of the family of Marion, and of their ancient arms, the charges of which—the three fleurs-de-lis—are the same as those now used by the representatives of the MAN OF ROSS.

LACY.—Two distinguished members of this ancient family, namely, Walter de Lacie, and Ilbert de Lacie, came into England with the Conqueror; but it has not been ascertained in what degree of relationship they stood to each other. WALTER was one of the Commanders whom WILLIAM sent into Wales to subjugate the principality; and being victorious, he acquired large possessions there, in addition to those already obtained, as his portion of the spoil of Hastings. These, vastly augmented by royal favour, and extensive grants in Ireland, descended, in the course of time, to Walter de Laci, " vir inter omnes nobiles Hiberniæ, eminentissimus," whose granddaughters and co-heiresses were Maud, wife of Peter de Geneva, and Margery, wife of John de Verdon. ILBERT DE LACI, the fellow soldier, if not kinsman, of Walter, had, from his Royal Master, a grant of the castle and town of Brokenbridge, Yorkshire, which he afterwards denominated, in the Norman dialect, Pontefract. From him sprang the De Lacys, Constables of Chester, and Earls of Lincoln, whose last male-heir, Henry de Lacy, third Earl of Lincoln, and *jure uxoris* Earl of Salisbury, one of the most eminent noblemen of his time, died in 1312, " at his mansion-house, called Lincoln's Inn, in the suburbs of London, which he himself had erected," leaving an only daughter and heir, ALICE, Countess of Lincoln and Salisbury, who married, first, Thomas Plantagenet, Earl of Lancaster, secondly, Eubold de Strange, and thirdly, Hugh le Frenes; but died without issue. The curious privilege, " the patronage of the minstrels," which was enjoyed by the Duttons, had its origin in the services of Roger de Lacy, Constable of Chester (great grandfather of the last Earl of Lincoln.) In his time, Ranulph, Earl of Chester, having entered Wales, at the head of some forces, was compelled by superior numbers, to shut himself up in the castle of Rothelaw, where, being closely besieged by the Welsh, he sent to De Lacy, Constable of Chester, who forthwith marched to his relief, at the head of a concourse of people then collected at the fair of Chester, consisting of minstrels and loose characters of all descriptions, forming altogether so numerous a body, that the besiegers, at their approach, mistaking them for soldiers, immediately raised the siege. For this timely aid, the Earl conferred upon de Lacy and his heirs the patronage of all the minstrels in those parts; which patronage the Constable transferred to his Steward Dutton, and his heirs The privilege was—" that at the Midsummer Fair, held at Chester, all the minstrels of that country resorting there, do attend the heir of Dutton, from his lodging to St. John's Church (he being then acccompained by many gentlemen of the country), one of them walking before him in a surcoat of his arms depicted on taffata; the rest of his fellows proceeding two and two, and playing on their several sorts of musical instruments. When divine service terminates, the like attendance upon Dutton to his lodging, where a court being kept by his Steward and all the minstrels formerly called, certain orders and laws are made for the government of the society of minstrels."

LATIMER.—This surname is said to have been adopted from the tenure of certain lands, which required the possessor thereof to act as "latimer," or *interpreter*. In English history it occupies a prominent place, and has been borne at various times by the most distinguished warriors. In the reign of Henry III. flourished WILLIAM DE LATIMER, a crusader under Prince Edward, and a gallant soldier in the French wars; and under Edward III., William, Lord Latimer, his great grandson, a warrior of great renown, celebrated for a victory achieved over Charles of Blois, at the siege of Doveroy, where, with only 1600 men, English and Bretons, he encountered that Prince, who had come to the relief of the place at the head of 3,600 men; and defeated and slew him, besides nearly a thousand knights and esquires; taking prisoners also, two earls, twenty-seven lords, and fifteen hundred men-at-arms. The only child and heiress of this heroic soldier was ELIZABETH LATIMER, married, 1st, to John, Lord Nevill, of Raby; and 2nd, to Robert, Lord Willoughby de Eresby. Another branch of the house of Latimer were the Lords Latimer of Braybroke, whose eventual representative (in the female line), EDWARD GRIFFIN, was created in 1688 Baron GRIFFIN of BRAYBROKE.

LOVEDAY.—A family of this name, bearing for arms "per pale arg. and sa, an eagle displayed with two heads, counterchanged; armed, membered, and ducally gorged or," is seated at Williamscote, co. Oxford, being now represented by JOHN

LOVEDAY, Esq., High Sheriff of the county in 1841.

LOVELL.—Robert, Lord of Breherval and Yvery in Normandy, a younger son, it is stated, of Eudes, sovereign Duke of Brittany, was the potent noble to whom this entry on the Roll of Battle Abbey refers. He received from the Conqueror a grant of the Lordships of Kary and Harpetre, in the county of Somerset; but returned eventually to his native Duchy; where he assumed the cowl, and died a monk in the abbey of Bec, leaving three sons, of whom the eldest, Ascelin Gouel de Perceval, succeeded his father as Lord of Breherval. This feudal chief held, like his predecessor, a distinguished place in the Norman army, and was rewarded for his services with divers manors, particularly Weston and Stawel, co. Somerset. He was a man of violent temper, and thence acquired the surname of "Lupus." Ordericus Vitalis gives the particulars of a long and extraordinary dispute which Ascelin had with the Earl of Bretevil, and which ended by his obtaining his own terms, after sustaining a seige of two months, in his castle of Breherval, against a powerful army, commanded by the ablest captains of the age, which terms included the retention of the fortress, and the hand of Isabella, the Earl of Bretevil's only daughter, in marriage. The issue of the union thus accomplished, were seven sons and one daughter. Of the former, the eldest, Robert, Earl of Yvery, died *s. p.* in 1121, and was *s.* by his brother WILLIAM, surnamed "Lupellus," or the little wolf, which designation was softened into *lupel*, and thence to *luvel*. By Auberice, his wife, sister of Walleran de Bellemonte, Earl of Mellent, William Lupellus had five sons; 1st, WALERAN, Lord of Yvery in Normandy; 2nd, RALPH, Lord of Castle Kary, in Somersetshire, died *s. p.*; 3rd, HENRY, ancestor of the Lords Lovel of Kary, whose heiress, Muriel Lovel, *m.* Sir Nicholas St. Maur, Lord St. Maur; 4th, William, ancestor of the LOVELS of Tichmersh; and 5th, Richard, who retained the original surname of Perceval, and from whom descended the EARLS OF EGMONT. The Lovels of Tichmersh, who had summons to Parliament, 26th January, 1297, were a baronial family of considerable distinction. The last baron, Francis, 9th Lord Lovel of Tichmersh, created Viscount Lovel, in 1483, was an eminent military commander, and is said to have fallen at the battle of Stoke, fighting in support of the pretensions of Lambert Simnell. The circumstance, however, of his lordship's death at Stoke admits of doubt, for after the battle he was certainly seen endeavouring on horseback, to swim the river Trent; yet, from this period, no further mention is made of him by any of our historians. A rumour prevailed that he had, for the time, preserved his life, by retiring into some secret place, and that he was eventually starved to death, by the treachery or negligence of those in whom he had confided; which report seems, in later days, to be confirmed by a very particular circumstance related in a letter from William Cowper, Esq., clerk of the Parliament, concerning the supposed finding of the body of Francis, Lord Lovel:—

Hertingfordbury Park, 9 Aug. 1737.
Sir,—I met t'other day with a memorandum I had made some years ago, perhaps not unworthy of notice. You may remember, that Lord Bacon, in his history of Henry VII., giving an account of the battle of Stoke, says of the Lord Lovell, who was among the rebels, that he fled and swame over the Trent on horseback, but could not recover the further side, by reason of the steepnesse of the bank, and so was drowned in the river. But another report leaves him not there, but states that he lived long after in a cave or vault. Apropos to this; on the 6th of May, 1728, the present Duke of Rutland related in my hearing, that about twenty years then before—viz. in 1708, upon occasion of new laying a chimney at Minster Luvel, there was discovered a large vault under ground, in which was the entire skeleton of a man, as having been sitting at a table, which was before him, with a book, paper, pen, &c.; in another part of the room lay a cap, all much mouldered and decayed, which the family and others judged to be the Lord Lovel, whose exit has hitherto been so uncertain.
W. COWPER.

Hence it may be inferred that this once powerful but ill-fated nobleman retired secretly to his own castle; and having entrusted himself to some friend or dependant, died either by treachery or neglect—a melancholy period to the fortunes of one of the greatest and most active personages of the era in which he flourished. In his lordship vested the baronies of Lovel, Holland, D'Eyncourt, and Grey of Rotherfield, all of which fell under the attainder that closed the last act of his life's tragedy. One of Lord Lovel's manors—that of Bayons, co. Lincoln, has become, by subsequent grant and re-purchase, the property of the right Honourable CHARLES TENNYSON D'EYNCOURT, who descends from the heir-male of this distinguished warrior.

LUCY.—The first mention of the family of Lucy is in a render made by King Henry I. of the lordship of Dice, in Norfolk, to Richard de Lucie, governor of Falais, who subsequently acted a prominent part in the contests of Stephen's reign, and was more than once LIEUTENANT OF ENGLAND.—The affinity which existed between that celebrated noble and Reginald de Lucie, the ancestor of the Lords Lucy, whose heiress Maud, wedded Henry Percy, first Earl of Northumberland, Dugdale declares his inability to discover. The Lucys of Charlecote, co. Warwick (Shakespeare's Lucys), now represented by HENRY SPENSER LUCY, Esq., descend from Sir William de Charlecote, who changed his name to Lucy, from the fact, it is supposed, of his mother being the heiress of some branch of the great baronial family of Lucy.

LASCALES —This Norman adventurer seems to have been requited for his services by grants in the Northern Counties, particularly in Yorkshire, where his descendants were seated at a very early period. Dugdale states that the family produced divers persons of great note many ages since;—the chief of whom was ROGER DE LASCELS, summoned to Parliament as a baron, *temp.* EDWARD I. From this ancient stock, the Earls of Harewood claim descent.

LOTERELL.—In the reigns of Henry I. and Stephen, Sir J. Luttrell (son or grandson probably of the Norman warrior) held, *in capite*, the manor of Hoton Pagnel, in Yorkshire, which eventually devolved upon an heiress, who married John Scott, feudal Lord of Calverley, and Steward of the household to the Empress Maud. Of the derivative branches were the feudal barons of Irnham, the EARLS OF CARHAMPTON and the LUTTRELLS of Dunster, co. Somerset.

LONGUEUALE.—The descendants of the Norman Longueville became Lor ls of Overton. co. Huntingdon, and Wolverton, Bucks; and in one branch vested the barony of Grey de Ruthin. During the great civil war, they arrayed themselves under the royal banner, and suffered, in consequence, loss and confiscation. The chief of the house, Sir Edward Longueville, of Wolverton, was created a baronet of Nova Scotia by Charles I. His grandson, Sir Thomas Longueville, last Bart., was seated at Prestatyn, co. Flint, and Esclusham, co. Denbigh. He married Maria Margaretta, dau. of Sir John Conway, Bart., and left three daughters, his co-heirs, viz.: 1. Maria Margaretta, who *m.* 1st, Thomas Jones; 2nd, Joseph Taylor, gent., by the former of whom she was grandmother of Thomas Longueville Jones, Esq., of Prestatyn, who took the name of Longueville, and of Hugh Jones, Esq., of Lark Hill, West Derby, co. Lancaster; 2nd. Conway, who *m.* George Hope, Esq., and died *s. p.*; and 3rd, Harry, *m.* to the Rev. Richard Williams, of Cron, co. Flint.

LANE, or DE LA LONE.—From this Norman the Lanes of Staffordshire claim descent, a family illustrious in history for the part they took in the preservation of King Charles II. After the battle of Worcester, Col. John Lane, the head of the house, received the fugitive Prince at his mansion of Bentley, whence his Majesty was conveyed in disguise by the Colonel's eldest sister, Jane Lane, to her cousin Mrs. Norton's residence near Bristol. This loyal lady married in the sequel Sir Clement Fisher of Packington, in Warwickshire, and received, after the Restoration, an annual pension of £1000 for life. From her brother, the cavalier Col. Lane (to whom it was granted, in augmentation of his paternal coats, an especial badge of honour, viz. the arms of England in a canton, with, for *crest*, a strawberry roan horse, bearing between his fore legs the Royal Crown), lineally descends the present JOHN NEWTON LANE, Esq., of King's Bromley Manor, co. Stafford.

LOVETOT.—Not long after the Conquest, we find William de Lovetot possessed of Hallam, Attercliffe, Sheffield, and other places in Yorkshire, and we subsequently trace his family, for three generations, as feudal Lords of Hallamshire. Little attention has been paid by our genealogists to the origin of this potent house, but certain it is that its benign influence laid the foundation of the prosperity which that district of Yorkshire enjoys to this day. The feudal chieftain of the time of our early Norman Kings in his baronial hall, presents not at all times an object which can be contemplated with satisfaction by those who regard power but as a trust, to be administered for the general good. With authority little restricted by law or usage, he had the power of oppressing as well as benefiting the population by which he was surrounded, and many doubtless were the hearts which power so excessive seduced. It is gratifying when we find those who could overcome its seductive influence. And such seem to have been the family of De Lovetot. Few of their transactions have come down to us, but none which leave a blot upon their memory, and some which shew that they had a great and humane regard for the welfare of those whom the arrangements of Providence had made more immediately dependant on them. One of their first cares was to plant churches on their domains, and their religious zeal is still further displayed by the foundation and endowment of the splendid monastery of Worksop. The last of the male line of the Lovetots, William, Lord of Hallamshire, died between the 22nd and 27th years of the reign of Henry II., leaving an only daughter, Matilda or Maud, then of very tender age. This lady was heir to her father's large possessions, and, through her mother, was nearly allied to the great house of Clare. Her wardship fell to the king, but Henry seems to have left it to his son and successor, Richard Cœur de Lion, to select the person to whom her hand should be given, and therefore to appoint to what new family the fair lordship of Sheffield should devolve. As might be expected, Richard chose the son of one of his companions in arms; and Maud de Lovetot was bestowed on Gerard de Furnival, a young Norman knight, son of another Gerard de Furnival, distinguished at the siege of Acre. Thus the Furnivals became possessed of the Lordship of Hallamshire, which eventually passed, through the marriage of their heiress, to the Talbots, Earls of Shrewsbury, and from them to the Howards, Dukes of Norfolk.

MALET.—William, Lord Malet de Greville, was one of the great barons who accompanied the Conqueror, and had, in charge, to protect the remains of the fallen monarch, Harold, and to see them decently interred after the battle. His son, Robert, Lord Malet, possessed at the general survey, thirty-two Lordships in Yorkshire, three in Essex, one in Hampshire, two in Notts, eight in Lincolnshire, and two hundred and twenty-one in Suffolk. The near kinsman of this Robert,

William Malet, Lord of the Honour of Eye in Suffolk, was one of the subscribing witnesses to Magna Charta; and from him lineally derives the present SIR ALEXANDER MALET, Bart., of Wilbury House, Wilts.

MALHERBE.—The descendants of this knight were seated at Fenyton in the county of Devon, as early as the reign of Henry II., and continued there for thirteen generations, when the heiress married Ferrers, and afterwards Kirkham. The arms of the Malherbes were, *or a chev. gu. between three nettle leaves erect ppr.*, referential to the family name.

MAUNDEVILLE.—Upon the first arrival in England of the Conqueror, there was amongst his companions a famous soldier, called Geffray de Magnavil, so designated from the town of Magnavil in the Duchy of Normandy, who obtained as his share in the spoil of conquest, divers fair and wide spreading domains in the counties of Berks, Suffolk, Middlesex, Surrey, Oxford, Cambridge, Herts, Northampton, Warwick, and Essex. The grandson of this richly gifted noble, another GEOFFREY DE MANDEVILLE, was advanced by King Stephen to the Earldom of Essex, but nevertheless, when the Empress Maud raised her standard, he deserted his Royal benefactor, and arrayed himself under the hostile banner. In requital the Empress confirmed to him the custody of the Tower of London, granted the hereditary Sheriffalty of London, Middlesex, and Herts, and bestowed upon him all the lands of Eudo Dapifer in Normandy, with the office of steward, as his rightful inheritance, and numerous other valuable immunities, in a covenant witnessed by Robert, Earl of Gloucester, and several other powerful nobles, which covenant contained the singular clause, " that neither the Earl of Anjou, the Empress's husband, nor herself, nor her children, would ever make peace with the burgesses of London, but with the consent of him the said Geoffrey, because they were his mortal enemies." Besides this, he had a second charter, dated at Westminster, recreating him Earl of Essex. Of these proceedings King Stephen, having information, seized upon the Earl in the court, then at St. Albans, some say after a bloody affray, in which the Earl of Arundel, being thrown into the water with his horse, very narrowly escaped drowning; certain it is, that to regain his liberty the Earl of Essex was constrained, not only to give up the Tower of London, but his own Castles of Walden and Blessey. Wherefore, being transported with wrath, he fell to spoil and rapine, invading the king's demesne lands and others, plundering the abbeys of St. Albans and Ramsay: which last having surprised at an early hour in the morning, he expelled the monks therefrom, made a fort of the church, and sold their religious ornaments to reward his soldiers; in which depredations he was assisted by his brother-in-law,

William de Say, a stout and warlike man, and one Daniel, a counterfeit monk. At last, being publicly excommunicated for his many outrages, he besieged the Castle of Burwell, in Kent, and going unhelmed, in consequence of the heat of the weather, he was shot in the head with an arrow, of which wound he soon afterwards died. This noble outlaw had married Rohesia, daughter of Alberic de Vere, Earl of Oxford, Chief Justice of England, and had issue, Ernulph, Geoffrey, William, and Robert; and by a former wife, whose name is not mentioned, a daughter Alice, who married John de Lacy, constable of Chester. Of his death, Dugdale thus speaks:—
"Also that for these outrages, having incurred the penalty of excommunication, he happened to be mortally wounded at a little town called Burwell; whereupon, with great contrition for his sins, and making what satisfaction he could, there came at last some of the Knights Templars to him, and putting on him the habit of their order, with a red cross, carried his dead corpse into their orchard, at the old Temple, in London, and coffining it in lead hanged it on a crooked tree. Likewise, that after some time, by the industry and expenses of William, whom he had constituted Prior of Walden, his absolution was obtained from Pope Alexander III., so that his body was received among Christians, and divers offices celebrated for him; but that when the prior endeavoured to take down the coffin and carry it to Walden, the Templars being aware of the design, buried it privately in the church-yard of the NEW TEMPLE, viz. in the porch before the west door."

William de Mandeville, last surviving son of this famous noble, succeeded as third Earl of Essex, at the decease of his brother Geoffrey, and not long after made a pilgrimage to the Holy Land. At his death, which occurred in 1190, the feudal lordship and estates he enjoyed devolved on his aunt Beatrix, wife of William de Say; and from her, passed to the husband of her grand-daughter—the celebrated Geoffrey Fitz-Piers, Justice of England, whom Matthew Paris characterizes as "ruling the reins of government so, that after his death, the realm was like a ship in a tempest without a pilot." His only daughter and eventual heiress, Maud, wedded Robert de Bohun, Earl of Hereford, and had a son, Humphrey de Bohun, Earl of Hereford and Essex, with whose male descendants the latter Earldom continued until the decease, in 1372, of Humphrey de Bohun, Earl of Hereford, Northampton, and Essex, whose elder daughter and co-heir, Alianore, married Thomas of Woodstock, Duke of Gloucester, sixth son of Edward III., and was mother of Anne Plantagenet, the consort of William Bourchier, Earl of Ewe, in Normandy. Of this alliance, the son and heir, Henry Bourchier, Earl of Ewe, obtained a patent of the Earldom of Essex in 1461, and was succeeded therein by his grandson,

Henry Bourchier, second Earl of Essex, at whose demise, in 1539, the representation of his illustrious house and of the Mandevilles and Bohuns, Earls of Essex, devolved on his sister, Cicely, wife of John Devereux, Lord Ferrers of Chartley, whose great-grandson, Walter Devereux, second Viscount Hereford, was raised in 1572 to the Earldom of Essex, a title that expired with Robert Devereux, third Earl, the Parliamentary General. It was, however, revived in about fifteen years after in the person of Arthur, Lord Capel, whose wife, the Lady Elizabeth Percy, was granddaughter of Lady Dorothy Devereux, sister of Robert, Earl of Essex, the favourite of Queen Elizabeth. Thus the present Earl of Essex can deduce an unbroken line of descent through each successive family that held the honour, from Geoffrey de Mandeville, upon whom the Earldom of Essex was conferred by King Stephen.

MARMYON.—The chiefs of this great house are stated to have been hereditary champions to the Dukes of Normandy, prior to the Conquest of England: certain it is, that Robert de Marmyon, Lord of Fonteney, obtained from his royal master, not long after the battle of Hastings, a grant of the manors of Tamworth, co. Warwick, and Scrivelsby, co. Lincoln, the latter to be held " by the service of performing the office of champion at the King's Coronation." His descendants and eventual co-heiresses were Joan Cromwell, wife of Alexander Lord Frevile, and Margaret de Ludlow, wife of Sir John Dymoke, between whom his estates were partitioned, Frevile receiving Tamworth, and Dymoke, Scrivelsby, with the championship of England, which is still held by his descendant, Sir HENRY DYMOKE, Bart. of Scrivelsby.

MALEUILE.—The great Northern House of Melville claims this Norman as the patriarch of their race. Galfrid de Maleville, the earliest of the family who appears in Scottish history, had the honour of being the first Justiciary of Scotland on record. From him derived the Earls of Melville.

MARTEINE.—This entry on the Battle Abbey Roll refers to the famous Martin de Tours, who came over from Normandy with the Conqueror, and was distinguished at the battle of Hastings. Subsequently he acquired by conquest, as one of the Lords Marcher, a large district in Pembrokeshire, called Cemaes or KEMES, and became Palatine Baron thereof, exercising within his territory, subject to feudal homage to the King, all the *jura regalia* which, at that period, appertained to the crown of the English monarch. He made Newport the head of his Palatinate, and there erected his castle, the ruins of which still exist. From this potent noble, the Palatine Barony of Kemes has descended to the present THOMAS DAVIES LLOYD, Esq., Bronwydd, co. Cardigan, who derives from Martin de Tours, through the families of Owen of Henllys, and Lloyd of Penpedwast. He holds the lordship by the same tenure, and exercises the *jura regalia* in the same manner as his great ancestor did under the Conqueror. Newport, the "caput baroniæ," has been, time immemorial, under the local jurisdiction of a mayor (appointed annually by Mr. Lloyd of Bronwydd,) and twelve burgesses: courts leet and baron are held at stated periods in the town, where all the business of the lordship is transacted, fresh grants of land given by the burgesses, under the sanction of the lord, and other affairs settled. The lordship is fifty miles in circumference, and each farm in it pays what is called a "chief rent" to Mr. Lloyd, of Bronwydd. He is obliged to walk the boundaries every five years, a task which generally occupies a week.

The immediate male descendants of Martin de Tours were summoned to parliament in the Barony Martin, which, at the decease of William, Lord Martin, in 1326, fell into abeyance between his heirs, Eleanor Columbers, his sister, and James de Audley, his nephew, as it still continues with their representatives.

MARE.—The descendants of this Norman knight occupied a prominent position in Staffordshire, in the time of the early Plantagenets. William de Mere occurs as High Sheriff of that county, *temp.* Edward II., and in the next reign, Peter de la Mere filled the speaker's chair in the House of Commons. At an early period, the family possessed the manor of Maer, co. Stafford, and are also found resident at Norton, in the Moors.

The name is spelt, in ancient deeds, de Mere, de Mare, but the more recent orthography is Mayer.

MAULEY.—The first of this name we can trace is Peter de Mauley, a Poictevin, Baron of Mulegrave, and Lord of Doncaster, in Yorkshire. He appears to have been an adherent of King John, and to have acquired his English estates in marriage with Isabel, daughter and heir of Robert de Thurnham, whose wife was Joanna Fossard, heiress of Mulgrave, a descendant, probably, of the Domesday Nigel. Camden says, that "by marriage Peter de Mauley came to a great inheritance at Mulgrave, and that the estate was enjoyed by seven Peters, Lords de Malo-lacu, successively, who bore for arms "or, a bend sa." But the seventh, who had summons to parliament from 22 Ric. II. to 3 Hen. V., dying *s. p.*, his possessions were divided between Sir John Bigot, Knt., and George Salvaine, of Duffield, who had married his sisters. The manor of Mulgrave is now the property of the Marquis of Normanby.

MORTIMER.—Ralph de Mortimer, supposed to have been son of the famous Norman general, Roger de Mortimer, and to have been related to the Conqueror, held a principal command at the battle of Hastings; and, shortly after, as the most puissant of the victor's captains, was sent into the Marches of Wales to encounter Edric, Earl of Shrewsbury, who still resisted the Norman yoke. This nobleman, after much difficulty and a long seige in his castle of Wigmore, Mortimer subdued, and delivered into the king's hands; when, in requital of his good services, he obtained a grant of all Edric's estates, and seated himself at Wigmore. Thus arose, in England, the illustrious house of Mortimer, destined to occupy the most prominent place on the roll of the Plantagenet nobility, and to transmit to the royal line of York a right to the diadem of England, which, after the desolating contests of the Roses, triumphed in the person of Edward, Earl of March, who ascended the throne as fourth of his name. Roger, Lord Mortimer of Wigmore, so notorious in our histories as the paramour of Queen Isabel, was grandson of Roger Mortimer, the illustrious adherent of Henry III. in the baronial war, to whom Prince Edward was indebted for his deliverance from captivity after the battle of Lewes. The exploit is thus recorded by Dugdale:—"Seeing his Sovereign in this great distress, and nothing but ruin and misery attending himself, and all other the king's loyal subjects, he took no rest till he had contrived some way for their deliverance; and to that end sent a swift horse to the prince, then prisoner with the King in the castle of Hereford, with intimation that he should obtain leave to ride out for recreation, into a place called Widmersh; and that upon sight of a person mounted on a white horse, at the foot of Tulington Hill, and waving his bonnet (which was the Lord of Croft, as it was said), he should haste towards him with all possible speed. Which being accordingly done (though all the country thereabouts were thither called to prevent his escape), setting spurs to that horse, he overwent them all. Moreover, that being come to the park of Tulington, this Roger met him with five hundred armed men; and seeing many to pursue, chased them back to the gates of Hereford, making great slaughter amongst them." At the ignominious death, on the common gallows, of Roger Mortimer, Queen Isabel's favourite, his earldom of March became forfeited, but was restored to his grandson, Roger, Lord Mortimer, a warrior of distinction and a Knight of the Garter. His son and successor, Edmund, Earl of March, espoused the Lady Philippa Plantagenet, daughter and heiress of Lionel, Duke of Clarence, and dying in 1381 (being then Lord Lieutenant of Ireland), left with two daughters, the elder, Elizabeth, wife of the gallant Hotspur, three sons, the eldest of whom, Roger, fourth Earl of March, was father of the Lady Anne Mortimer, who wedded Richard Plantagenet, Earl of Cambridge, and conveyed to the house of York the right to the Crown of England.

MONTRAUERS.—Although none of the family founded by this Norman knight were barons by tenure or had summons to parliament before the time of the third Edward, yet were they anciently persons of note. In the reign of Henry I., within less than half a century after the Conquest, Hugh Maltravers was a witness to the Charter made by that Monarch to the Monks of Montacute in the county of Somerset; and, in the 5th of Stephen, Maltravers gave a thousand marks of silver and one hundred pounds, for the widow of Hugh Delaval and lands of the said Hugh, during the term of fifteen years, and then to have the benefit of her dowry and marriage.

The infamous part which John, Lord Maltravers, took in the cruel murder of King Edward II., is too well known to need recitation here —enough is it to state that the wretched monarch was removed from the custody of Lord Berkeley, who had treated him with some degree of humanity, and placed under Lord Maltravers and Sir Thomas Gournay, for the mere purpose of destruction, and that those ruffians ultimately fulfilled their diabolical commission in the most horrible manner possible, in one of the chambers at Berkeley Castle. So conscious was Maltravers of guilt, that he fled immediately after the foul deed into Germany, where he remained for several years, having had judgment of death passed upon him in England; but in the 19th of the same reign, King Edward being in Flanders, Lord Maltravers came and made a voluntary surrender of himself to the King, who, in consideration of his services abroad, granted him a safe convoy into England to abide the decision of parliament; in which he had afterwards a full and free pardon, (25 Edward III.), and was summoned as a BARON to take his seat therein. That was not, however, sufficient — King Edward constituted the murderer of his father, soon after, Governor of the Isles of Guernsey, Alderney, and Sarke.

After the decease of this Lord Maltravers, the BARONY passed to his granddaughter (the eventual sole heiress of his predeceased son, Sir John Maltravers), Eleanor, wife of the Hon. John Fitz-Allan, whose son John was summoned to parliament as Lord Maltravers, and succeeded as eleventh Earl of Arundel, and the Barony of Maltravers has since merged in that superior dignity, Lady Mary Fitz-Allan, the daughter, and ultimately sole heiress of Henry, eighteenth Earl of Arundel, married Thomas Howard, Duke of Norfolk, and brought the barony and earldom into the Howard family. These dignities descended to her son Philip, who was ATTAINTED in the 32nd Elizabeth, when the barony fell under the attainder, but it was restored to his son, Thomas Howard, twentieth Earl of Arundel; and by Act of Parliament, 3rd Charles I., the BARONY OF MALTRAVERS, together with those of Fitz-Allan, Clun, and Oswaldestre, was annexed to the title, dignity, and honour of ARUNDEL, and settled upon Thomas Howard, then Earl of Arundel.

MOUNTAGU.—The Christian name of the distinguished soldier to whom this entry refers, was Drogo, denominated "de Montagu," from a town in Normandy. In Domesday Book, he is styled Drogo de Montacuto, and appears by the possessions he held under Robert, Earl of Morton, to have come over in the retinue of that great Earl, the half-brother of the Conqueror. This Drogo fixed his chief residence at the castle of Shipton-Montacute, co. Somerset, and hence his descendants continued to be designated. Simon de Montacute, Lord of Shipton-Montacute, gained great distinction as a successful warrior in the martial times of Edward I. "In the 24th of that monarch" (says Hollinshed) "those Englishmen that kept the town of Burg, being compassed about with a siege by Monsieur de Sully, obtained a truce for a certain space; during the which, they sent unto Blaines for some relief of vittels, and where other refused to bring up a ship laden with vittels, which was there prepared, the Lord SIMON DE MONTAGEW, a right valiant chieftaine, and a wise, took upon him the enterprise, and thro' the middle of the French gallies which were placed in the river to stop, that no ship should passe towards that towne; by help of a prosperous wind, he got into the haven of Burg, and so relieved them within of their want of vittels; by means whereof, Monsieur de Sulley broke up his siege and returned into France." From this renowned soldier descended the illustrious race of Montague, conspicuous in all the great achievements of English history. Thomas de Montacute, last Earl of Salisbury, was concerned in so many military exploits, that to give an account of them all would be to write the annals of the reign of Henry V. Suffice it then to say, that as he lived, so he died, in the service of his country; being mortally wounded when commanding the English army at the siege of Orleans, in 1428. His wife was the Lady Eleanor Holland, a descendant of the royal house of Plantagenet, and by her he had an only daughter and heiress, the Lady Alice, who wedded Richard Nevill, eldest son of Ralph, Earl of Westmoreland, by his second wife, Joane de Beaufort, dau. of John of Gaunt. In right of this marriage, Richard Nevill had the Earldom of Salisbury revived in his person, and was succeeded therein by his eldest son, Richard Nevill, Earl of Warwick and Salisbury, the hero of the Wars of the Roses,

"The setter-up and puller down of Kings."

Though the chief line of the Montacutes thus failed in an heiress, male branches continued to flourish, and from these sprang the Dukes of Montague and the Earls of Halifax, now extinct, the Dukes of Manchester, and the Earls of Sandwich.

MOUNTFORD.—Hugh de Montfort, commonly called "Hugh with a Beard," son of Thurstan de Bastenburgh, accompanied William from Normandy, and aided that prince's triumph at Hastings, for which eminent service he obtained divers fair lordships; and at the time of the

General Survey was possessor of twenty-eight in Kent, sixteen in Essex, fifty-one in Suffolk, and nineteen in Norfolk. The descendant of this fortunate soldier, PETER DE MONTFORT, living *temp*. Henry III., became one of the most zealous amongst the turbulent barons of the era, and, after the battle of Lewes, was of the *Nine* nominated to rule the kingdom; in which station he enjoyed and exercised more than regal power, but of short duration, for he fell at the subsequent conflict of Evesham, so disastrous to the baronial cause. His male line terminated with his great-grandson, Peter de Montfort, third lord, who died *s. p.* in 1367, leaving an illegitimate son, SIR JOHN MONTFORT, Knight, whose posterity flourished in the male line for several subsequent generations at Coleshill, co. Warwick, until the attainder of Sir Simon Montfort, Knt., *temp*. Henry VII., whose descendants continued at Bescote, co. Stafford.

MAULE.—The ancient Norman family of Maule assumed their surname from the town and lordship of Maule, in the Vexin Francois, eight leagues from Paris. Roger, last Lord of Maule, was slain at the battle of Nicopolis in Hungary, fighting against the Turks, anno 1398, and his coat of arms was set up in the Parisian Cathedral of Notre Dame. His only daughter and heir married Simon de Morainvillers, Lord of Flaccourt. A cadet of this eminent family, Guarin de Maule, a younger son of Ansold, Lord of Maule, accompanied the Conqueror to England, and acquired, as his portion of the spoil, the Lordship of Hatton, co York, with other extensive estates. His son, Robert de Maule, attaching himself to David, Earl of Huntingdon, afterwards David II., removed into Scotland with that monarch, and obtained broad lands in Lothian, whereon his descendants became seated, until the thirteenth century, when the marriage of Sir Peter de Maule with the richly-dowered heiress of William de Valoniis, brought into the family the Barony of Panmure, ever after the chief designation of the Maules. Of this alliance the issue was two sons, SIR WILLIAM DE MAULE, ancestor of the Lords Panmure, and SIR THOMAS DE MAULE, Governor of Brechin Castle, the only fortress that interrupted the conquests of Edward I.

MONTHERMER.—Ralph de Monthermer, who is described as "a plain Esquire," married the Lady Joan Plantagenet, daughter of King Edward I., and widow of Gilbert Earl of Clare and Gloucester, and had the title of Earl of Gloucester and Hertford in her right. Probably this Ralph was a descendant of the Knight whose name appears in the Battle Roll. His grand-daughter and heiress, Margaret de Monthermer, wedded Sir John de Montacute, and conveyed the Barony of Monthermer to the family of Montacute.

MAINELL. — Hugo de Grante

Mesnill was one of the most potent Barons of the Conquest. His descendants were summoned to parliament in the reign of Edward I., and possessed vast estates in the Midland Counties and in Yorkshire. The Meynells of Hoar Cross, co. Stafford, and of Langley, co. Derby, claim to derive their lineage from Hugo de Grante Mesnill.

MALEVERER.—Sir Richard Mauleverer, Knight, came into England with the Conqueror, and was constituted Master or Ranger of the Forests, Chases, and Parks north of the Trent. He was founder of the family of MAULEVERER of Arncliffe, co. York.

MONHAUT.—Eustace de Monte Alto, surnamed the Norman Hunter, was one of the soldiers of the Conquest, in the immediate train of the Palatine Earl of Chester, the potent Hugh Lupus, from whom, in requital of his gallant services, Monte Alto or Monhaut obtained the Lordships of Montalt and Hawarden in Flintshire, places still designating a branch of his descendants, the noble house of Maude, Viscounts Hawarden and Barons of Montalt. Eustace's great-great-grandson, Andomar de Montalt, founded the Yorkshire and only surviving line of the family. His eldest brother, Robert de Montalt, who received summons to parliament from 27 Edward I. to 13 Edward III., died *s. p.* Andomar, accompanying, in 1174, the expedition against William the Lion, had the good fortune to make the Scotch monarch prisoner by surprise; and conveying the royal captive to Henry II., then at Falaise, that prince granted to him, instead of his ancient insignia, "a Lion gu (the Lion of Scotland) debruised by two bars sa," to denote captivity. From his son and heir, Robert de Montalt, descended the Maudes of West Ryddylsden, the parent stem, from which sprang the Maudes, now Lords Hawarden, and the Maudes of Alverthorpe-hall, near Wakefield (connected in marriage with the Lowthers of Lowther Castle,) whose senior representative, resident in Yorkshire, is the present JOHN MAUDE, of Moor-house, Esq., a Magistrate and Deputy Lieutenant of the West Riding, the author of a most interesting and graphic work, published at Wakefield in 1826, under the title of "A Visit to the Falls of Niagara in 1800."

MINERS.—This gallant Norman appears to have been rewarded by grants of lands in Herefordshire. Certain it is that the estate of Treago in that county has been held by the family of Mynors from the era of the Conquest even to the present day, being now possessed by PETER RICKARDS MYNORS, Esq., who represents also the great and historic house of Baskerville of Erdesley, and derives in direct descent from the royal line of Plantagenet.

MOUNTGOMERIE.—Roger de Montgomerie was kinsman of William of

Normandy, and commander of the first body of the Duke's army at the battle of Hastings. There is an old MS. at Grey Abbey, co. Down, written about the year 1696, by William Montgomery, of that place, son of the Hon. Sir James Montgomery, giving an account of this family, in which he remarks: "For the honour of the nation in general, let it be known to all, that there is at this day the title of a Counte or Earle of the name of all his Majesty's four kingdoms; viz., Count Montgomery, in France; Earl of Montgomery, in England; Earl of Eglinton, in Scotland; and Earl of Mount Alexander, in Ireland; the like whereof cannot be truly said (as I believe) of any other surname in all the world." In the same manuscript, he states, alluding to ROGER, fifth Count de Montgomery, who led the van at the battle of Hastings—"In anno 1652, I saw in Westminster Abbey, this ROGERS' coat of arms and name written under it, as benefactor of the building thereof. He was in rank or place the seventh or eighth (as I remember) among the contributors to the said building, or to the convent thereof; but in anno 1664, I found that his name or arms, and all the rest (above forty noblemen's), were wholly razed out as writings (on a stone table book) are with a wet sponge."

MAINWARING. — Ranulphus de Mesnilwarren was the name of the Norman adventurer thus recorded on the Battle Roll. He received the grant of fifteen lordships, including Over Peover, and founded the family of Mainwaring, so distinguished in the annals of Cheshire. The chief line, that of Peover, was raised to a baronetcy at the Restoration in 1660, but the title became extinct at the death, in 1797, of the late Sir Henry Mainwaring, who devised his estates to his uterine brother, Thomas Wetenhal, Esq. The present male representative of this ancient house is Captain ROWLAND MAINWARING, R.N., of Whitmorehall, co. Stafford.

MORTON.—Cardinal Morton, Archbishop of Canterbury and Lord Chancellor, *temp.* Henry VII., was probably a descendant of the Norman knight. Of this celebrated prelate, Anthony Wood states, "that he was a wise and eloquent man, but in his nature harsh and haughty —that he was much accepted by the king, but envied by the nobility and hated by the people. He won the king's mind with secrecy and diligence, chiefly because he was his old servant in his less fortunes, and for that also he was in his affections not without an inveterate malice against the house of York, under which he had been in trouble." From the Cardinal's brother, Richard, descended the Mortons of Milbourne St. Andrew, co. Dorset, raised to the degree of baronets in 1619, and now represented by the Pleydells.

NOEBS.—This name should, we think, be written Noels, and must apply to the patriarch of the eminent family of Noel. Be this, however, as it may, evident it is, from the foundation of the Priory of Raunton, in Staffordshire, that Noel came into England with the Conqueror; and, for his services, obtained the manors of Ellenhall, Wiverstone, Podmore, and Milnese. His eldest son, Robert Noel, Lord of Ellenhall, was further enriched, *temp.* Henry I., by a grant of the greater part of Gainsborough, from the Prior of Coventry. This potent Lord founded the monastery of Raunton, in Staffordshire. From him derived the Noels of Hilcote, and the Noels of the counties of Rutland and Leicester. Sir Andrew Noel, Knight, of Dalby, in the last-named shire, was a person of great note in the reign of Elizabeth, living in such magnificence as to vie with noblemen of the largest fortune. Fuller, in his "Worthies," saith that this Andrew, "for person, parentage, grace, gesture, valour, and many other excellent parts (amongst which skill in music), was of the first rank in the Court." He was knighted by Queen Elizabeth, and became a great favorite; but the expenses in which he was involved, obliged him to sell his seat and manor of Dalby, a circumstance which elicited from the Queen the following distich upon the imprudent knight's name:

"The word of denial and letter of fifty,
Is that gentleman's name who will never be thrifty."

Sir Andrew's son and successor, Edward, Lord Noel, of Ridlington, succeeded his father-in-law, Baptist Hickes, in the Viscountcy of Campden, and died in the garrison of Oxford, 10th March, 1643, leaving a son and heir, Baptist Noel, Viscount Campden, a devoted adherent of the royal cause, and a severe sufferer in consequence, his princely seat in Gloucestershire having been burnt down by the King's forces to prevent its becoming a garrison to the Parliamentarians. His Lordship's eldest son, Edward Noel, Viscount Campden, was raised, in 1682, to the Earldom of Gainsborough, a dignity that expired in 1798, at the death of Henry Noel, sixth Earl, whose grand-nephew, Charles Noel Noel, Lord Barham, had the old title of his maternal ancestors revived in his person, and is the present Earl of Gainsborough.

The Noels of Kerby Mallory, co. Leicester, were a younger branch of the Ridlington Noels. Their senior representative is Anna Isabella, the Dowager Lady Byron.

NEVIL.—Gilbert de Nevil, the companion in arms of the Conqueror, is styled by some genealogists the Duke's Admiral; but in the General Survey no mention of any person of the name occurs. Gilbert's grandson, Geoffrey de Nevil, wedded Emma, daughter and heir of Bertram de Bulmer, Lord of Brancepeth, and left a son, Henry, who died, *s. p.*, in 1227, and an only daughter, Isabella, the greatest heiress of her time, who became the wife of

Robert Fitz-Maldred, Lord of Raby, the lineal male representative of Uchtred, Earl of Northumberland. Out of gratitude for the large inheritance brought to them by the heiress of Nevill, or in compliance with the fashion of the time to *Normanize*, the Saxon Lords of Raby thenceforward assumed the appellation of Nevill, and from that period the fortunes of the family rapidly culminated, till they eclipsed, by their more recent splendour, the Saxon honours of the house. From "a Sketch of the Stock of Nevill," by W. E. Surtees, Esq., D.C.L., we extract the following able summary of the most illustrious race on the roll of English genealogy :—

"To John Lord Nevill, who was at different periods warden of the East Marches, Governor of Bamborough, High Admiral of England, Lieutenant of Aquitaine, and Seneschal of Bourdeaux, is to be chiefly attributed the building of the splendid pile of Raby, which in 1379, he had a license to castellate. In 1385, he attended Richard II. on his expedition to Scotland. The nobility of the north formed the rearward, and Lord Nevill's train consisted of two hundred men-at-arms, and three hundred archers. He died at Newcastle-on-Tyne, in 1388, and lies buried in Durham cathedral, where his altar-tomb still remains between the pillars of the south aisle.

"His son and successor, Ralph Lord Nevill, was created Earl of Westmoreland, 17 Richard II. He soon afterwards deserted (together with Henry Percy first Earl of Northumberland) the falling fortunes of Richard, and was one of the principal instruments in placing the House of Lancaster on the throne. The new monarch showered dignities on the family of Nevill. The Earl was invested in the honour of Richmond, and made Earl Marshal: and by his second marriage—that with Joan, daughter of John of Gaunt, 'time-honour'd Lancaster '—became brother-in-law to his sovereign. When the Percys revolted, he adhered faithfully to Henry. On his side he fought at the battle of Shrewsbury; on the eve of which, to this greeting given to Sir Richard Vernon by Hotspur,

'My cousin Vernon! Welcome by my soul!'

Vernon answers :—

'Pray God my news be worth a welcome, lord. The Earl of Westmoreland, seven thousand strong,
Is marching hitherwards; with him Prince John ;'

thitherwards to that field from which soon the gallant young Percy

'Threw many a northward look to see his father
Bring up his powers; but he did look in vain,'

ere the dubious victory of the rebels was changed, by his own death, to a ruinous defeat.

"In a second insurrection in the North, he was the ' well-appointed leader' who, being sent, together with Prince John, with an inferior force against the rebels, dispersed their army, without bloodshed, at

Shipton Moor, near York, and delivered up their chiefs, Mowbray and Scrope, Archbishop of York, to Henry and the scaffold. Some say that he effected this by deceiving the simplicity of the aged prelate in agreeing to his proposals; others that he persuaded him to disband his followers, as the only means of appeasing the King and procuring a favourable answer to his petitions.

"In the next reign he followed Henry V. into France, and shared in the victory of Agincourt. With the discrimination of character which Shakspere invariably exhibits, Westmoreland, the veteran experienced warrior, recommends Henry to subdue first his troublesome neighbours on the other side the Tweed:—

'For once the eagle England being in prey,
To her unguarded nest the weasel Scot
Comes sneaking, and so sucks the princely eggs.'

"In the roll of Agincourt the Earl Marshal had in his train five knights, thirty lances, and eighty archers. Of these, the names of some strike familiarly on a northern ear, as Sir Thomas Rokesby, Sir John Hoton, Edmond Rodham, Roger Ratcliffe, John Swinborne, John Wardale, John Wytton.

"Shakspere preserves the consistency of his character by making him wish, as any reasonable man would do before the commencement of so doubtful a battle,—

'Oh that we now had here,
But one ten thousand of those men in England
That do no work to-day.'

While Henry, with real or assumed romantic feeling, answers:—

'The fewer men the greater share of honour.'

"The strong light in which Shakspere brings out Westmoreland in his Henry IV. and Henry V., is a proof that he was even then remembered as a subtle and powerful agent in the intrigues of his age. He died full of years and honours in 1426, and is buried under 'a right stately tomb of alabaster' in the choir of his own collegiate church of Staindrop. The Earl had twenty-one children. From his first bed sprung the Earls of Westmoreland. But none of his descendants in this, the elder line, seem to have inherited his talent or his ambition.—From his second bed arose the princely house of Salisbury, Warwick, and Montague, whose blood mingled with that of Plantagenet, and the Lords Fauconberg, Latimer, and Abergavenny."

OLIFANT and OLIFARD.—The first of the descendants of this Norman, occurring in the public records, was DAVID OLIFARD, who served in the army of King Stephen in 1141. A conspiracy was formed against the Empress Maud, who escaped from Winchester, attended by David I. Surrounded by the enemy, the Scottish King owed his safety to the exertions of his godson Olifard, who, although in the adverse party, aided his Royal opponent. In recompense, the rescued Monarch gave to his preserver, who settled in North Britain, the Lands of Crailing and Smallham in Roxburghshire, and conferred on him the dignified office of Justiciary. Thus was established the famous family of Oliphant, so distinguished in the annals of Scotland. Among its early members, Sir William Oliphant, of Aberdalgy, the gallant defender of Stirling Castle against Edward I., stands prominently forward. Stirling, under Oliphant, was the last fortress that remained in the hands of the Scots. Edward laid siege to it in 1304; every engine known in those days was employed in the attack. The King, though far advanced in years, exposed his person with the fire and temerity of a young soldier. The defence was obstinate and bloody. All the works were ruined, many breaches made, the ditch filled up, and the Castle reduced to a heap of rubbish. The siege commenced 22nd April; in July, Sir William Oliphant sought to capitulate; the King would listen to no terms, and the Garrison was obliged to surrender at discretion, 20th July following. The sixth in descent from this knightly warrior was LAURENCE, LORD OLIPHANT, ancestor of the noble House of Oliphant, the Oliphants of Gask, the Oliphants of Condie, &c.

PIGOT.—In an elaborate MS. compiled and emblazoned in the College of Arms, containing "sundrie ancient remembrances of arms genealogies, and other notes of gentility belonging to the worshipful name and families of Pigot or Picot," it is stated that "in the first reign of the Normans, there flourished in this land two noble families of the surname of Pigot; and that they were of the like noble lineage or offspring in the Duchy of Normandy before the Norman Conquest of England, appeareth by the reverend testimonies of our ancient Heralds' books and chronicles: the first whereof being named otherwiles Pigot and Picot, was Viscount Hereditary of Cambridge Sheer, or Grantbridge, and Baron of Boorne, or Brune, in the said county, in the reign of King William the Conqueror. After his death, Robert Pigot, his son, succeeded in the Baronie, and he forfeited the same by taking part with Robert, Duke of Normandy, against William Rufus; and King Henry the First gave the same to Payne Peverell. This Peverell married the sister of the said Lord Robert Pigot, as Mr. Camden noteth in his description of Cambridgeshire.

"The other family of the Pigots that is said to have been of noble title about the Conqueror's time, did flourish in the west parts of the realm, namely, in Wales, on the Marches thereof, as it seemeth. For Humphry Lloyd, and Doctor Powell, in their Chronicles of Wales, p. 167, affirm that in the reign of King Henry the First, A.D. 1109, Cadogan-ap-Blethin, Lord of Powys, married the daughter of the Lord Pigot of Say, a nobleman of Normandie, and had divers towns and lordships in that countrie by gifts of the said Pigot, and a son also by his daughter, named Henry, to whom the King gave a portion of his uncle Ierworth's ransome, which Ierworth-ap-Blethin was the said King's prisoner.

"It is supposed from a branch of this Pigot are lineally descended those PIGOTT's which have many ages since continued at *Chetwin*, in *Shropshire*, their arms being three fuzills or millpecks, as aforesaid; likewise in Flintshire, Cheshire, Herefordshire, &c., whereof there are many gentleman remaining in Wales to this day, as is reported and known."

Of the Cheshire branch of Pigot, it is known by authentic records, that Gilbert Pigot or Pichot was mense Lord of Broxton at a period approximating to the Norman Conquest. Robert Pigot, and William, his son, by charter granted to the monks of St. Werberg, in Chester, the town of Chilleford; and another Gilbert Pigot was a benefactor to the Abbey of Pulton, in that county, in the year 1210.

RICHARD PIGOT, of "Cheshire," presumed to have been of the family of Pigot of Butley, in that county, and to have descended from Gilbert, Lord of Broxton, before mentioned, married the daughter and co-heiress of Sir Richard de Peshale, of Chetwynd, in the county of Salop, and with her obtained that fine estate.

PIERREPOINT.—Although the family of PIERREPOINT did not attain the honours of the Peerage until a period of comparatively recent date, yet were they persons of distinction ever since the Conquest. In which eventful era, ROBERT DE PIERREPOINT was of the retinue of William, Earl of Warren, and at the time of the General Survey, held lands in Suffolk and Sussex amounting to ten knights' fees, under that nobleman. The great grandson of this Robert, another ROBERT DE PIERREPOINT, was a person of such extensive property, that, being made a prisoner fighting on the side of King Henry III. at the battle of Lewes, he was forced to give security for the payment of the then great sum of seven hundred marks for his ransom. He was, however, relieved from the obligation by the subsequent victory of the royalists at Evesham. He was *s.* by his son, Sir HENRY DE PIERREPOINT, a person of great note at the period in which he lived. In the 8th of Edward I., Sir Henry having lost his Seal, came into the Court of Chancery, then sitting at Lincoln, upon Monday, the morrow of the Octave of St. Michael, and made publication thereof; protesting, that if any one should find it, and seal therewith after that day, that the instrument sealed ought not to be of any validity. He *m.* Annora, daughter of Michael, and sister and heir of Lionel de Manners, whereby he acquired an extensive property in the county of Nottingham, with the Lordship of Holme, now called HOLME-PIERREPOINT.

His direct descendant, ROBERT PIERREPOINT, was advanced to the Peerage, by King Charles I., as

BARON PIERREPOINT, of Holme, Pierrepoint, in the county of Nottingham, and VISCOUNT NEWARK, by letters patent, dated 29th June, 1627, and the next year was created EARL OF KINGSTON-UPON-HULL.

At the breaking out of the Civil War his Lordship was one of the first and most zealous to espouse the royal cause, and he is said to have brought no less than four thousand men immediately to the standard of the King. He was soon after constituted Lieutenant-general of His Majesty's Forces in the counties of Lincoln, Rutland, Huntingdon, Cambridge and Norfolk; and was amongst the most popular of the Cavalier commanders. His Lordship became, therefore, an object of more than ordinary watchfulness to the Parliamentarians, and was at length surprised and made prisoner by Lord Willoughby, of Parham, at Gainsborough, whence he was despatched in an open boat towards Hull.

The last male representative of this distinguished race, Evelyn Pierrepoint, second Duke of Kingston (whose wife was the notorious Duchess of that name), died in 1773, when his estates devolved on his nephew, Charles Medows, Esq., afterwards created Earl Manvers.

PRENHIRLEGAST.—This name is generally supposed to be synonymous with Prendergast, which family, soon after the Conquest, held possessions in the county of Pembroke, and at Akill, in Northumberland, which last estate its owners forfeited in 1327, by their adherence to the Scottish party. Maurice, Lord of Prendergast, near Pembroke, was one of the most eminent of Strongbow's companions in the conquest of Ireland.

Although, by Henry the Second's orders he returned to England in 1175, and carried thence the rebellious Robert, Earl of Essex, captive into Normandy, yet, in 1177, he again landed in Ireland, and in that country his descendants have ever since remained. One branch held Ferns and Enniscorthy, with the Garteens and other large estates in Wexford, forfeited in 1641. The elder line held Newcastle Prendergast, in Tipperary, from the conquest of Ireland, until the death of Thomas Prendergast, at the beginning of the 17th century. He had married, Eleanor, sister to Walter, eleventh Earl of Ormonde, and aunt of the celebrated Duke of Ormonde. His children were deprived of their vast possessions by Cromwell, which were restored to them by a Decree of Innocency in 1660, to be again lost in 1689.

The present Viscount Gort, who uses the additional surname of Prendergast, is heir general of this ancient family, whilst the male still flourishes in the persons of the gallant Major General Sir Jeffrey Prendergast, and Thomas G. Prendergast, of Johnstown Park, in Tipperary, Esq.

POWER —The immediate descendant of the Norman Le Poer, or

Power, was SIR ROGER LE POER, Knt., who accompanied Strongbow to Ireland, and obtained for his services three considerable territorial grants. Of Sir Roger, Crambensis writes with high encomium. He was ancestor of the Lords de la Poer, now represented by the MARQUESS of WATERFORD, and the many eminent families of Power in the South of Ireland, the Powers of Clashmore, Faithlegg, Kilfane, Belleville, &c.

PAINELL.—Sir John Paynell of Drax, co. York, was summoned to Parliament as a Baron, from 29th Dec. 1299, to 25th Aug. 1318.

PECHE.—The Barons Peche, of Brunne, co. Cambridge, summoned to Parliament, *temp.* EDWARD I., and the Barons Peche, of Wormleighton, summoned in the succeeding reign, appear to have been the representatives of the Norman Peche.

PEVERELL.—" William, the Conqueror of England" (we quote no less an authority than 'the Author of Waverley,') " was, or supposed himself to be, the father of a certain William Peveril, who attended him to the battle of Hastings, and there distinguished himself. The liberal-minded monarch, who assumed in his charters the veritable title of ' Gulielmus Bastardus,' was not likely to let his son's illegitimacy be any bar to the course of his royal favour, when the laws of England were issued from the mouth of the Norman victor, and the lands of the Saxons were at his unlimited disposal. William Peveril obtained a liberal grant of property and lordships in Derbyshire, and became the erector of that Gothic fortress, which, hanging over the mouth of the Devil's Cavern, so well known to tourists, gives the name of Castleton to the adjacent village. From the feudal Baron, who chose his nest upon the principles on which an eagle selects his eyry, and built it in such a fashion, as if he had intended it, as the Irishman said of the Martello towers, for the sole purpose of puzzling posterity, there was, or conceived themselves to be, descended (for their pedigree was rather hypothetical,) an opulent family of knightly rank, in the same county of Derby. The great fief of Castleton, with its adjacent wastes and forests, and all the wonders which they contain, had been forfeited in King John's stormy days, by one William Peveril, and had been granted anew to the lord Ferrars of that day. Yet this William's descendants, though no longer possessed of what they alleged to be their original property, were long distinguished by the proud title of the Peverils of the Peak, which served to mark their high descent, and lofty pretensions." The details of the Norman Peveril, as given by the Romaucist, are strictly correct, and we need merely add, that William de Ferrars married the heiress of William Peveril, the younger.

PEROT.—WILLIAM, was surnamed "DE PERROTT," from Castel Perrott, which he built in Armorica (Brittany), and the town of Perrott, one league from it. He came over to England in 957, and obtained some lands in Wessex, on a river which changed its name to the Perrot (now corrupted to the Parret), in Somersetshire; but was constrained to return to Armorica, and his grandson, the SEIGNEUR DE PERROTT, in Brittany (who m. Blanche, dau. to Ramyro, 2nd King of Arragon, and nearest relative of Norman William), furnished the CONQUEROR with his quota of ships and men, and came over with him; for which, with other services in the field he was knighted by the duke. Sir Richard then went to take possession of the lands his forefather held in Somersetshire, and began there a city, whose remains are North and South Perrott. His son, SIR STEHHEN PERROTT, m. the celebrated Princess Ellyn, Lady of Jestynston, dau. of Howel Dha, the great King of all Wales, "the Lycurgus or lawgiver of that land." The valour and magnanimity of Sir Stephen gained him the respect and love of the Princess Ellyn's people. Their son, Sir Andrew, claimed the kingdom of Wales, in right of his mother, and collected a body of forces in assertion of his right, but the King of England marched a numerous army into the country to take advantage of the disorders; the knowledge of which and a sum of money offered by the English king, through the Bishop of St. David's, brought him to declare for that prince, who knighted him, on his doing homage for the land for twenty miles round Sir William's camp, whereon he built the Castle of Narbeth, whose ruins are extant in Pembroke. He m. Jonet, dau. of Ralph, Lord Mortimer. by Gladdis Dee, dau of Llewellyn, (the last of the Welsh princes, and who was slain in fighting for his dominions against EDWARD I.) Lord Mortimer's mother was Maud, dau. of WILLIAM the Conqueror.

In the direct line of their descendants were many knights-banneret, (as well as the celebrated William (Perrott) *de* Wykeham, Bishop of Winchester); one of them, Sir Thomas, m. Alice Picton, who was of the first blood of one of the knights of the Garter, Sir Guy de Bryan, by which the Barony of Laughane and other heritages came to the Perrotts. It was by the advice of their grandson, Sir Owen, that HENRY VII. landed at Milford, where he assisted the claimant to the crown of England with men and money; so nearly was he related to the king (both by Tudor and Plantagenet affinity), that the Royal letters styled Sir Owen "our dearly beloved cousin." The present representative of the Norman Perot appears to be SIR EDWARD BINDLOSS PERROTT, Bart.

POMERAY.—The ancient family of Pomeray founded by the Norman continued to possess the Barony of Berry, co. Devon, until the attainder of Sir Thomas Pomeroy in the reign of Edward VI. They had intermarried with heiresses or co-heiresses of Vallefort, Merton, Bevill, and Denzell. The eldest line became extinct *temp*. Queen ELIZABETH, when the heiress is said to have married Penkevil. Younger branches were of Sandridge and Ingeston, Devon, and of Pallice, co. Cork. Samuel Pomeroy, Esq., the representative of the Irish line, left six daus., his co-heirs, viz., Rebecca, *m.* to Francis Drew, Esq., of Kilwinny and Meanus; Martha, *m.* to Robert Holmes, Esq.; Mary, *m.* to Abraham Lecky, Esq.; Susanna, *m.* to Capt. Thomas Campion; Sarah, *m.* to Daniel Webb, Esq.; and Elizabeth, *m.* to the Rev. John Jones, D.D.

PLUKENET.—Little of certainty is to be gathered concerning this name before its appearance in Ireland. So early, however, as the 11th century, we find John Plukenet seated at Beaulieu, co. Meath: and from him springs the distinguished Irish families of the name, ennobled under the titles of Fingall, Dunsany, and Louth.

PERCELAY OR PERCY.—William de Percy, Lord of Percy, near Villedieu, accompanied Duke William from Normandy, and, being high in favour with his victorious master, obtained, according to Madox, in his "Baronia Anglica," a barony of thirty knights' fees. This Lord William de Percy, who was distinguished amongst his contemporaries by the addition of Alsgernons (William with the Whiskers), whence his posterity have constantly borne the name of Algernon, restored or rather refounded the famous abbey of St. Hilda, in Yorkshire, of which his brother, Serlo de Percy, became first prior. Accompanying, however, Duke Robert in the first crusade, 1096, he died at Mountjoy, near Jerusalem, the celebrated eminence whence the pilgrims of the cross first viewed the holy city, leaving four sons and two daus. by his wife, Emma de Port, a lady of Saxon descent, whose lands were amongst those bestowed upon him by the CONQUEROR, and according to an ancient writer, "he wedded hyr that was very heire to them, in discharging of his conscience." His lordship was *s.* in his feudal rights and possessions by his eldest son, ALLEN DE PERCY, second baron, surnamed the GREAT ALLAN; who *m.* Emma, dau. of Gilbert de Gaunt, and was *s.* by his eldest son, WILLIAM DE PERCY, third baron; at whose decease the eldest branch of the first race of Percys, from Normandy, became extinct in the male line, and their great inheritance devolved upon his lordship's two daughters, the LADIES MAUD and AGNES DE PERCY, successively:

MAUD DE PERCY, the elder, was first wife of William de Newburgh, Earl of Warwick, by whom (who *d.* in the Holy Land, A.D. 1184) she had no issue. Her Ladyship *d.* in 1204-5, and then the whole possessions of the Percys descended to the family of her sister,

AGNES DE PERCY, who *m.* Josceline, of Lovain, brother of Queen ADELICIA, second wife of HENRY I., and son of Godfrey Barbatus, Duke of Lower Lorrain, and Count of Brabant, who was descended from the

Emperor CHARLEMAGNE. Her Ladyship would only consent, however, to this great alliance upon condition that Josceline should adopt either the surname or arms of Percy; the former of which he accordingly assumed, and retained his own paternal coat, in order to perpetuate his claim to the principality of his father, should the elder line of the reigning duke, at any period, become extinct. The matter is thus stated in the great old pedigree at Sion House: "The ancient arms of Hainault this Lord Jocelyn retained, and gave his children the surname of Perci." Of this illustrious alliance there were several children; of whom, Henry, the eldest son, was ancestor of the Percies of Northumberland, a race not more famous in arms than distinguised for its brilliant alliances—a race, whose renown, coeval with its nobility, has flourished in every age and co-existed with every generation since.

The banner of the present Duke of Northumberland exhibits an assemblage of nearly nine hundred armorial ensigns; among which, are those of King Henry VII., of several younger branches of the Blood Royal, of the Sovereign Houses of France, Castile, Leon, and Scotland, and of the Ducal Houses of Normandy and Brittany, forming a galaxy of heraldic honours altogether unparalleled.

PERCIVALE.—Robert, Lord of Breherval, in Normandy, and his son Ascelin Gouel de Percival, both fought under the Norman banner at Hastings, and both obtained many extensive manors in the conquered country. Ascelin wedded Isabella, daughter of William, Comte of Yvery, and was himself established in that Earldom, A.D. 1119. His second son, William Gouel de Percival, Earl of Yvery, was father of five sons, viz., 1. Waleran, ancestor of the Barons of Yvery in Normandy, II. Ralph, Baron of Karvy, III. Henry, also a Baron, IV. William, ancestor of the Lord Lovel, and V. Richard Sir Knight, Lord of Hawell, Patriarch of the Lords Percival of Ireland, the Percivals of Tykenham, co. Somerset, and the Earls of Egmont, with the various derivative branches.

QUINCY.—In the reign of the Second Henry, Saier de Quincy had a grant from the crown of the Manor of Bushley, co. Northampton, previously the property of Anselme de Conchis. Of his two sons, the elder, Robert, became a Soldier of the Cross, and the younger, Saier, was created Earl of Winchester by King John. He subsequently obtained large grants and immunities from the same monarch, but, nevertheless, when the Baronial War broke out, his Lordship's pennant waved on the side of freedom, and he became so eminent amongst his contemporaries that he was chosen one of the twenty-five Barons appointed to enforce the observance of Magna Charta. His adventurous career was at length terminated in 1219, when he died on his way to Jerusalem, after participating at the Siege of Damieta. His granddaughter and eventual co-heirs were Margaret, wife of William de Ferrers, Earl of Derby, Elizabeth, *m.* to Alexander Comyn, Earl of Buchan, and Elab, *m.* to Alan, Lord Zouch of Ashley.

Ros.—In the reign of Henry I., Peter, Lord of Ros, in Holderness, assumed the local surname, and founded the great Baronial family of Ros of Hamlake, which, by an intermarriage with the daughter and heiress of William de Albini, acquired Belvoir Castle in Leicestershire, an inheritance still enjoyed by the Duke of Rutland, a descendant of the tenth Baron Ros of Hamlake. The old Barony now vests in William-Lennox-Lascelles-Fitzgerald, Lord de Ros.

Ridel.—Almost all the versions of the Battle Abbey Roll include the name of Ridel; and Thierry, in his "Histoire de la Conquête de l'Angleterre par les Normands," further specifies that "Ridel" was among the Norman conquerors. By reference to the first volume of "Pipe Rolls," edited by Mr. Stapleton, it will be seen at p. 119, that Geoffrey Ridel rendered accompt for himself and for Geoffrey de St. Denis of forty shillings for two copes. It was by this tenure that the fief of Blosseville in the pays de Caux, was held, which gave to the possessor in later times the title of Vicomte hereditaire, Chatelain et Seigneur Haut Justicier de Blosseville. This entry proves that the Ridels originally existed in Normandy. The first of the race, explicitly proved to have been settled in Scotland, is Gervasius Ridel, the earliest High Sheriff of Roxburghshire. From him derives the present Sir Walter Buchanan Riddell, Bart., of Riddell, co. Roxburgh. The Norman Ridel was ancestor also of the eminent Northumbrian House of Riddell of Fenham and Swinburne Castle, now represented by Thomas Riddell, Esq., of Felton Park.

Rous.—Radulphus le Rufus, a knight in the train of the Conqueror, was grandfather of William le Rufus, one of the Justices Itinerant of the Counties of Wilts, Dorset, Somerset, Devon, and Cornwall, *temp.* Henry II. From this eminent person derived the Rous's of Edmerston and Halton, co. Devon, of whom was the famous Francis Rous, Speaker of the Short Parliament. The present male representative of the family is Thomas Bates Rous, Esq., of Courtyrala, co. Glamorgan.

Rochford.—The family, descended from the Norman Rochford, styled in old deeds and writings, *De Rupe forti*, was established in Ireland at the time of, or soon after, the first invasion of the English, for so early as 27th Henry III., we find Sir Richard de Rochfort, and John de Rochfort, Lords of Crom and Adare. In 1302, Sir Maurice Rochfort was Lord Justice of Ireland; and in 1309, lived Sir Milo de Rochfort, who was direct ancestor of the Rochforts of Belvedere, Rochfort, and Clogrenane.

SOUCH. — That the Zouches branched from the Earls of Brittany is admitted by all genealogists, but they do not coincide in the exact line of descent.

SENCLERE.—The family of Senclere or Sinclair, (de Sancto claro) migrated within less than a century after the arrival in England of its patriarch, the Norman Senclere, to North Britain, where it separated into two branches, the Sinclairs of Roslin, ancestors of the Earls of Orkney and Caithness, and the Sinclairs of Herdmanstoun, from whom sprang the Lords Sinclair.

SENT LEGERE.—Sir ROBERT SENT LEGERE, Knt., the companion-in-arms of the CONQUEROR, was, according to a tradition in the family, the person who supported that prince with his arm when he quitted the ship to land in Sussex. This Sir Robert, having overcome a pagan Dane who inhabited the manor of Ulcomb, in Kent, fixed his abode there; and in that place his posterity flourished for many generations. The lineal descendant of Sir Robert, SIR ARTHUR ST. LEGER, Knt., went first into Ireland in 1537, being appointed by Henry VIII. one of the commissioners for letting the crown lands there, and returning into England, was constituted lord-deputy of Ireland, 7th July, 1540. In 1543, he was recalled to inform the King of his administration of affairs; which gave his highness such satisfaction that he created him a knight-companion of the Garter, and sent him back lord-deputy, in which high office he continued until 1556, serving three sovereigns, when, being recalled by QUEEN MARY, he retired to his estate in Kent, and *d.* there, 12th March, 1559. This eminent person has been characterized "as a wise and wary gentleman, a valiant servitor in war, and a good justice in peace, properly learned, and having gravity interlaced with pleasantness." He *m.* Agnes, dau. of Hugh Warham, Esq., of Warham, and was *s.* by his second but eldest surviving son, SIR WARHAM ST. LEGER, of Ulcumb, who was appointed chief governor of Munster, in 1565, under the lord-deputy Sidney. In 1579, he was constituted knight-mareschal of the same province; and in 1580, he caused James of Desmond, who was denominated a notorious rebel, to be hanged under martial law at Cork. He was killed, eventually, in battle (in single combat), by Hugh Maguire, Lord of Fermanagh, who fell himself at the same time. Sir Warham *m.* Ursula, youngest dau. of George Nevil, Lord Abergavenny, and was *s.* by his son, SIR WILLIAM ST. LEGER, a privy councillor, and lord-president of Munster in 1627. Sir William represented the city of York in Parliament in 1639, and was appointed in that year sergeant-major-general in the army; he was subsequently employed against the rebels in Ireland; and dying about the year 1642, left, with other issue, from which descended the St. Legers of Yorkshire and Gen. St. Leger,

WILLIAM, his heir, slain at Newberry, 1644.

JOHN, successor to his brother, and ancestor of the Lords Doneraile.

Heyward, of Castlemore and Heyward's Hill, lieut.-col. in the army, and M.P.; ancestor of the present ANTHONY BUTLER ST. LEGER, Esq., of Heyward's Hill, co. Cork, and of his brother and heir-presumptive, HEYWARD JOHN ST. LEGER, Esq.

SENT QUINTIN.—Sir Herbert de St. Quintin, whose name appears on the Roll, came from Lower Picardy, where the chief town is called St. Quintin. His descendant, Herbert St. Quintin, summoned to parliament as a Baron, left a dau. and heiress, Lora, mother, by her third husband, Sir Robert Grey, of Rotherfield, of Elizabeth Grey, who m. Henry Lord Fitzhugh, and was direct progenitrix of Queen Catharine Parr.

SOMERVILLE.—The name of the Norman was Sir Gualter de Somerville. He became Lord of Whichnour, county Stafford, and his descendants possessed considerable property, about the close of the 12th century, in the co. Lanark, and in other parts of Scotland; of whom William de Somerville was one of the barons appointed at the marriage of ALEXANDER II. (whose reign commenced in 1214) to exercise in a tournament at the castle of Roxburgh. This William's descendant, James, thirteenth Lord Somerville, augmented his fortune considerably by an arrangement with his kinsman, William Somerville, Esq., of Eadstone, co. Warwick, and of Somerville-Aston, co. Gloucester, the celebrated poet, and author of the "Chase," representative of the English and elder branch of his lordship's family; by which, in consideration of certain sums applied to the relief of burdens, the poet, who was unmarried, settled the reversions of his estates upon Lord Somerville; and died in 1742, when the baron inherited accordingly. The present head of the family is Kenelm, LORD SOMERVILLE; a younger branch is represented, in the female line, by JAMES SOMERVILLE SOMERVILLE, Esq., of Dinder-house, co. Somerset.

SANFORD.—The family pedigree of the Sandfords, of Sandford, co. Salop, commences with Thomas de Sandford, the Soldier of the Conquest, who obtained as his part of the Spoliation, the lands of Sanford. Fuller, in the *Worthies of England*, observes—" This ancient name is still extant, at the same place in this county (Salop) in a worshipful equipage, for on the list of such as compounded for their reputed delinquency in our late civil wars, I find Francis Sandford, Esq., of Sandford, paying four hundred and fifty-nine pounds for his composition, yet I believe the gentleman begrudged not his money, in preservation of his own integrity, acting according to the information of his conscience and the practice of his ancestors. I understand that the said Francis Sandford was very well skilled in making warlike fortifications. The present chief of this ancient race is THOMAS HUGH SANDFORD, Esq., of Sandford, grandnephew of the late Daniel Sandford, Bishop of Edinburgh. A younger branch, that seated at the Isle of Up-Rossall, Shrewsbury, is represented by the Rev. HUMPHREY SANDFORD, M.A.

SOMERY.—In the reign of HENRY II., John de Somerie acquired the Barony of Dudley, in Staffordshire, by marrying Hawyse, sister and heir of Gervase Paganell. Their great-great-grandson, Sir John de Somerie who had summons to Parliament from 10th March, 1308, to the 14th March, 1322, died in the latter year, when his castles and lands devolved upon his sisters as coheirs, Margaret, the elder, married to John de Sutton, had the castles of Dudley and Joane, the younger, wife of Thomas Botetourt, had Rowley Somery, co. Stafford.

SENT JOHN.—WILLIAM DE ST. JOHN, whose name was derived from the territory of St. John, near Rouen, came into England with the CONQUEROR, as grand Master of the artillery, and supervisor of the waggons and carriages, whence the horses' hames, or collar, was borne for his cognizance. He m. Oliva, dau. of Ralph de Filgiers, of Normandy, and had by her, Thomas, who d. without issue, and JOHN DE ST. JOHN, who inherited, on the demise of his brother, all the lands in England, and principally the lordship of STANTON, co. Oxon (for distinction from the other towns of the same name, called STANTON ST. JOHN). This John was a person of great eminence in the reign of WILLIAM RUFUS, being one of the twelve knights that accompanied Robert Fitz-Hamon, Earl of Gloucester, in a warlike expedition against the Welsh, and received, "in reward for his great services, and helps in many victories," the castle of Faumont, co. Glamorgan. He had issue, a dau., Avoris, m. to Sir Bernard de St. Valery, and two sons—I. ROGER, ancestor of the noble House of ST. JOHN, and Thomas, Lord of Stanton, St. John, living 13 HENRY II., whose son, ROGER, was assessed £133 6s. 8d. for trespassing in the King's forests, 22 HENRY II. The grandson of this Roger, JOHN ST. JOHN, was killed at the battle of Evesham, 43 EDWARD III. He was in the holy wars with RICHARD I., who, at the siege of Acon, in Palestine, adopted the device of tying a leathern thong, or garter, round the left leg of a certain number of knights, (one of whom was this John St. John,) that they might be impelled to higher deeds of valour. This is supposed by some to have given the idea of the Order of the Garter.

SENT LES.—After the execution of Waltheof, the Conqueror offered Judith, his niece, the deceased Earl's widow, in marriage to SIMON ST. LIZ, a noble Norman, but the lady peremptorily rejected the alliance, "owing," Dugdale says, "to St. Liz's *halting in one leg;*" which refusal

B

so displeased the King, that he immediately seized upon the Castle and honour of Huntingdon, which the Countess held in dower, exposing herself and her daughters to a state of privation and obscurity in the Isle of Ely, and other places; while he bestowed upon the said Simon St. Liz, the town of Northampton, and the whole hundred of Falkeley, then valued at £40 per annum, *to provide shoes for his horses.* St. Liz thus disappointed in gaining the hand of the Countess of Huntingdon, made his addresses, with greater success, to her elder daughter, the Lady Maud, who became his wife, when William conferred upon the husband, the Earldom of Huntingdon and Northampton.

SENT GEORGE.—The descendants of Baldwin St. George, the Norman, flourished in England for several centuries, and frequently represented the County of Cambridge in parliament. They were seated at Hartley St George, in that shire, full 500 years. SIR RICHARD ST. GEORGE, Clarenceux king-of-arms, eighteenth in a direct line from Baldwin the Norman, *m.* Elizabeth, dau. of Nicholas St. John, Esq., of Lidiard Tregoze, co. Wilts, and had three sons,

I. Henry (Sir), Garter king-of-arms, who left four sons,
St. Thomas St. George, Garter king-of-arms.
Colonel William St. George, slain *ex parte regis.*
Sir Henry St. George, Clarenceux king-of-arms.
Sir Richard St. George, Ulster king-of-arms of Ireland.

II. George (Sir), of Carrickdrumrusk, co. Leitrim, whose grandson, SIR GEORGE ST. GEORGE, Bart., elevated to the peerage of Ireland, as LORD ST. GEORGE in 1715, left at his decease a dau., the Hon. Mary St. George, *m.* John Usher, Esq., M.P., by whom she had a dau., Judith, wife of George Lowther, Esq., of Kilrue, co. Meath, and a son, St. George Usher, who was elevated to the peerage of Ireland, in 1763, as LORD ST. GEORGE, *of Hartley St. George, co. Leitrim,* which dignity expired at his lordship's decease, without male issue, in 1775. His only dau., Emilia-Olivia, *m.* William-Robert, second Duke of Leinster.

III. Richard, who went over to Ireland, in the beginning of the 17th century, in the royal army, and was appointed governor of the town and Castle of Athlone. From him descend the four brothers, THOMAS BALDWIN ST. GEORGE, of Parsonstown, Acheson St. George, Esq., of Wood Park, co. Armagh, John St. George, Esq., of Woodside, Cheshire, and Archibald St. George, of Camma Lodge, co. Roscommon, as well as the Baronet of Woodsgift, the present SIR RICHARD BLIGH ST. GEORGE.

SAY—Picot de Say was, in the

time of the Conqueror, one of the principal persons in the county of Salop, under Roger de Montgomery, Earl of Shrewsbury, and founded the distinguished Baronial House of Say, from which derives, through female descent, the Lord Saye and Sele. Frederick Richard Say, Esq., of Harley Street, appears to be the male representative.

SENT BARBE.—Robert de St. Barbe, who came with the Conqueror from Normandy (in which province a town and two villages bearing the name are still to be found) was, according to an ancient charter of the Abbey of Glastonbury, progenitor of Robert St. Barbe of South Brent, co. Somerset, to whom the families of St. Barbe of Ashington, Whiteparish, and Ridgeway traced their pedigree. The only surviving branch is that settled at Lymington, Hants.

SENT MORE.—The baronial family of St. Maur, founded by the warrior of Hastings, became extinct in the chief male line at the decease in 1499 of Richard, 6th Lord St. Maur, whose only daughter and heiress, Alice, wedded William, 5th Lord Zouche of Haryngworth. The Seymours, Dukes of Somerset, whose historic greatness needs little of ancestral aid to augment its glory, claim to be a scion of the baronial house, and their pretensions may be sustained by the valuable authority of Camden.

TUCHET.—"The family of Touchet," says Collins, "hath been of great note, and came in with William the Conqueror, as is very evident, the name being on the Roll of Battle Abbey and in the Chronicles of Normandy." Its representative in the martial reign of Edward III. was Sir John Touchet, who married Joan, eldest daughter and eventually sole heir of James, Lord Audley of Heleigh, and thus secured to his descendants the inheritance of the ancient Barony of Audley, which is now enjoyed by George Edward Thicknesse Touchet, twentieth Lord Audley.

TRACY.—The Norman thus designated on the Roll, derived his name from the town of Traci, in his native Duchy. His descendants became Lords of Barnstaple in Devon, and enjoyed high repute in that county. Their heiress, Grace, only child of Henry de Traci, Baron of Barnstaple, *temp.* Henry I., married John de Sudeley, Lord of Sudeley and Toddington, and had two sons: RALPH, the elder, was ancestor of the Sudeleys, Lords of Sudeley Castle, whose eventual representative Joan, eldest sister and co-heir of John, Lord Sudeley, wedded Wm. Le Boteler, of Wem; and WILLIAM, the younger, took his mother's name of TRACI, and was possessed of Toddington, in Gloucestershire, and the Barony of Barnstaple, in Devon. He held twenty-six knights' fees in 1165, and was steward of Normandy. This William de Traci, it is asserted, was one of the murderers of Thomas à Becket. From him descended the TRACYS of TODDINGTON, VISCOUNTS

TRACY, of RATHCOOLE, and the TRACYS, BARONETS of STANWAY. Of the former, Henry Tracy, eighth Viscount, died in 1797, leaving an only dau. and heir, HENRIETTA SUSANNAH, m. in 1798, to Charles Hanbury, Esq., who assumed the additional surname and arms of Tracy, and was raised to the peerage in 1838, as Baron Sudeley. Since the decease in 1797, of the eighth Viscount Tracy of Rathcoole, the hereditary honours of the family have remained dormant, but they are now claimed by BENJAMIN WHEATLEY TRACY, Esq., Lieutenant R.N., and JAMES TRACY, Esq., who have both submitted their pretensions to the decision of the House of Lords.

TRUSSELL.—The Trussells were of knightly rank from their first establishment in England. The most distinguished personage of the name was the famous William Trussell, who was in such estimation with the Commons in convention assembled, as to be chosen their organ to pronounce the deposition of the unfortunate Edward II., which duty he executed in the following words:—

"Ego Wm. Trussell, vice omnium de Terrâ Angliæ et totius Parliamenti procurator, tibi Edwardo reddo homagium prius tibi factum et ex tunc diffido te, et privo omne potestate regia et dignitate, nequaquam tibi de cætero tanquam regi periturus."

The subsequent career of this distinguished statesman occupies a prominent place in the history of the eventful time in which he lived. At one period, an exile from the hostility of the Mortimers, he was at another the trusted favourite of the King, from whom he received the dignified office of Admiral of the Fleet, and had summons to Parliament as a Baron, 25th Feb., 1342. His Lordships seems to have left no descendants.

TALBOT.—Although some maintain that the illustrious family of Talbot was established in England antecedently to the Conquest, we cannot trace the fact by any authentic evidence. The first of the name occurring in the public records is, RICHARD DE TALBOT, one of the witnesses to the grant, which Walter Giffard, Earl of Buckingham, made to the Monks of Cerasie in Normandy, *temp.* Conquestoris. Richard de Talbot is also mentioned in Domesday Book, as holding nine hides of land from the said Earl of Buckingham. He married the daughter of Gerard de Gournay, Baron of Yarmouth, and had two sons, GEOFFREY, ancestor of the great House of TALBOT of BASHALL, co. York; and Hugh, who founded the still more illustrious family of TALBOT, ennobled under the title of Shrewsbury. The male line of the Bashall Talbots, whose chiefs were of knightly rank, and considerable historic importance, in the times of the Plantagenets and Tudors, terminated with THOMAS TALBOT, Esq., of Bashall, who died 25th Feb., 1618. His last surviving daughter and heir,

MARGERY TALBOT, wedded Colonel William White, of Duffield, co. Derby, and was mother of an only child, JANE WHITE, of Bashall, wife of Edward Ferrers, Esq., and mother of JOHN FERRERS, Esq., of Bashall, whose will was proved at York, 2nd October, 1707. The only son of this gentleman, William Ferrers, Esq., died unmarried, 23rd March, 1732, leaving his sisters his co-heirs. Elizabeth the younger was second wife of William Jodrell, Esq.; and DOROTHY, the elder, espoused Richard Walmesley, Esq., of Coldcoates Hall, co. Lancaster, by whom she was grandmother of MARGARET WALMESLEY, of Bashall, who married in 1766, Hugh Hughes Lloyd, Esq., of Plymog, co. Denbigh, and Gwerclas, co. Merioneth, and their grandson, RICHARD WALMESLEY LLOYD, Esq., is now representative of the TALBOTS of BASHALL. The younger, but more illustrious branch of this great name was, as we have already stated, that which became ennobled in the Earldom of Shrewsbury, and which has, for full six hundred years, acted a brilliant part in the annals of our country. The first Earl of Shrewsbury was Sir John Talbot, of the reigns of Henry V. and VI., one of the most illustrious characters in the whole range of English history. This renowned warrior, than whom

" A stouter champion never handled sword,"

was appointed, in 1412, lord-justice of Ireland, and in two years afterwards became lord-lieutenant of the same kingdom, in which important government he continued for seven years. He subsequently distinguished himself in the French wars of the fifth Henry, but his highest renown was attained upon the same field, in the reign of Henry VI., under the Regent John Plantagenet, Duke of Bedford, when his name alone became terrible, in consequence of the various successful expeditions he conducted. His lordship was attacked, however, by the MAID OF ORLEANS, at Patay, in 1429, and his army being entirely routed, he became captive to the enterprising and enthusiastic heroine. He was exchanged soon after for Ambrose de Lore, a celebrated French captain; and continuing to distinguish himself in arms, he was created, 29th May, 1442, EARL OF SHREWSBURY. His lordship was subsequently re-constituted lord-lieutenant of Ireland, and elevated to the peerage of that kingdom, 17th July, 1446, as *Earl of Waterford*, having been appointed at the same time lord-high-steward of Ireland. The Earl was now far advanced in life, but the English interests declining in France, he was once more induced to place himself at the head of the army there; and his courage and his conduct restored for some time at least its glory. He was nominated Lieutenant of the Duchy of Aquitaine, having under him, as Captains of his men-at-arms and archers, his son John Talbot, Viscount L'Isle, Sir John Hungerford,

Lord Molines, Sir Roger Camoys, Sir John L'Isle, and John Beaufort, the Bastard of Somerset. Marching immediately to the seat of his government, he took the city of Bourdeaux, and placed a garrison in it; whence, he proceeded to the relief of Chastillion, when an engagement with the French Army ensued, which terminated in the total defeat of the English, and the death of their gallant general, who was killed by a cannon ball. Thus fell, sword in hand, John Talbot, Earl of Shrewsbury, at the great age of 80, on the 20th July, 1453, after having won no less than forty pitched battles, or important rencontres. His remains were conveyed to England, and interred at Whitechurch, co. Salop, where a noble monument was erected in the south wall of the Chancel, with this epitaph:—

"Orate pro animâ prænobilis domini, domini Johannis Talbot, quondam Comitis Salopiæ, domini Furnivall, domini Verdon, domini Strange de Blackmere, et Mareschali Franciæ, qui obiit in bello apud Burdews, vij July, MCCCCLIII."

Few noble families can trace the acquisition of their coronets to such brilliant achievements as those of the illustrious Talbot. Suffice it to add that his descendants, even down to the present day, have not been unworthy of the name that has descended to them. Their present male representative is JOHN TALBOT, seventeenth EARL OF SHREWSBURY, and the heads of the different derivative branches are Charles Chetwynd, the present Earl Talbot, Sir George Talbot, Bart., and the Talbots of Lacock Abbey, Temple Guiting, &c. In Ireland, the principal family of the name is that of Talbot of Malahide, co. Dublin.

TOLLEMACH.—This must surely be a Monkish interpolation. The inscription in the old Manor-House of Bentley, in Suffolk—

"Before the Normans into England came,
Bentley was my seat, and Tollemache was my name,"

seems to set the matter at rest.

TOUKE.—Thoroton, in his "History of Nottinghamshire," states that the family of Toke was settled in that county as early as the reign of William Rufus. The pedigree given by that writer has the name spelled in seventeen different ways. Of this family was Sir Bryan Tuke, who was, first, Secretary to Cardinal Wolsey, afterwards, Foreign Secretary to Henry VIII, then, Treasurer of the King's Chamber, and finally, Ambassador to France, with Bishop Tunstall. From this eloquent and learned personage, described by Leland as "Anglicæ linguæ eloquentiæ mirificus," derived Sir Samuel Tuke of Cressing Temple, Essex, who was created a Baronet in 1663-4, and fell at the Battle of the Boyne. Other branches of the descendants of the Norman Touke became seated in the counties of Derby, Nottingham, York, Kent, Cambridge, Herts, Dorset, &c. Of the existing families, the chief is that of Godinton, in Kent, now represented by the REV. NICOLAS TOKE of that place.

The late Rev. William Tooke, F.R.S., author of the "History of Russia," derived his descent from the Tookes or Tokes of Hertfordshire, themselves scions of the Kentish stock. His sons, Thomas and William, now of London, are the well-known authors of several learned works.

TIBTOTE. — From this knightly warrior sprang the Lords Tibetot, summoned to parliament in 1803, and the Tiptofts, Earls of Worcester.

TURBEVILLE.—Within thirty years after the conquest, Sir Payn de Turbervill accompanied Sir Robert Fitz-Hamon, to the aid of Jestin-ap-Gwrgant, King of Glamorgan, against Rhys, Prince of South Wales. Subsequently, on the death of Rhys, Fitz-Hamon, turning his forces against Jestin, and conquering his whole dominion, divided it amongst his followers. To the share of Sir Payn de Turberville were allotted the castle and lordship of Coyty, and then was established in Wales the great house of Turbevill, seated at Coyty, Tythegstone, Penbline, Lantwitt Major, and Ewenny Abbey.

TURVILE —From which of the ten Seigniories of Tourville in the Duchy of Normandy the English Turviles came, cannot now be ascertained. Certain it is that William de Tourville accompanied Duke William to Hastings, and that soon after the conquest, the Tourvilles became extensive proprietors in the counties of Warwick and Leicester, giving in the latter their name to the manor of Normanton Turvile. The present representative is GEORGE FORTESCUE TURVILE, Esq., of Husband's Bosworth, co. Leicester.

TIRELL.—SIR WALTER TYRELL, a Norman knight, came into England, and soon after became tenant of the manor of Langham, co. Essex, which he held at the General Survey under Richard de Tonbrigg. Of this Sir Walter, Morant, in his History of Essex, observes: "Whether he was the same person who shot William Rufus in the New Forest, or whether he did it at the instigation of Archbishop Anselm, through the persuasion of a fanatic monk, as it is asserted by Alan de Insulis, we are not able to determine." It is far indeed from being an ascertained point that this was the Walter who slew Rufus, and as far is it from being certain that the deed was done designedly. Ordericus Vitalis, in his History of Normandie, relates, that Sir Walter Tyrell, on his death-bed, declared that he was not so much as in the field when William Rufus was killed. From Sir Walter Tyrell descended SIR THOMAS TYRELL, Knt., of Rumseys Tyrell, co. Essex, who *m.* Margaret, dau. of John Fillol, Esq., of Old Hall; and had issue two sons, JOHN (Sir), of Heron, whose son, JOHN TYRELL, Esq., of Springfield, in Essex, was created a Baronet in 1673, and Thomas of Battlebury, ancestor of the present Sir John Tyssen Tyrell, Baronet, of Boreham House, Essex.

VERE.—Alberic de Ver, the Norman Knight of the Conquest, is stated to have possessed numerous lordships in the different shires, of which Kensington, in Middlesex, was one, and Hedingham, in Essex, where his castle was situated and where he chiefly resided, another. From him descended the illustrious House of Vere, ennobled under the title of Oxford.

VERNOUN.—WILLIAM DE VERNON, who assumed that surname from the town and district of Vernon, in Normandy, of which he was proprietor in 1052, had two sons, RICHARD DE VERNON, and WALTER DE VERNON, who both came into England with WILLIAM the Conqueror. The elder, RICHARD, Lord of Vernon, was one of the barons created by Hugh Lupus, Earl of the County Palatine of Chester, by the title of Baron of Shipbroke. This Richard, who, according to Domesday-Book, was a considerable landed proprietor, was *s.* at his decease by his eldest son, WILLIAM DE VERNON, whose great-grandson, RICHARD DE VERNON, had a grant, in the 37th of HENRY III., of the castle and manor of Pecke; and dying before his father, left four sons, whereof

> WARINE, who *s.* his grandfather as Baron of Shipbroke, *m.* Auda, dau. and co-heir of William Malbank, Baron of Wich-Malbank, now Namptwich, co. Chester, with whom he acquired several manors in that shire, and by whom he had two sons, WARINE and Ralph. He was *s.* by the elder.
>
>> WARINE, Baron of Shipbroke, who *m.* Margaret, dau. of Ralph de Andeville, and relict of Hugh de Altaribus, by whom he had a son, WARINE, (who *d. s. p.*) and three daus., his co-heirs, viz.,
>>
>>> MARGERY, *m.* to Richard de Wilbraham.
>>> EDITH, *m.* to Sir William Stafford, Knt.
>>> ROHESIA, *m.* to John Littlebury.
>>> These ladies, after a prolonged litigation with their uncle, RALPH, were obliged to surrender to him a moiety of their patrimony. The son of this Ralph, Sir Ralph de Vernon, is said to have lived to the age of 150, and thence was generally called the OLD LIVER.

And

SIR WILLIAM DE VERNON, Knt., of Harlaston, in the co. of Stafford (the 3rd son), was chief-justice of Chester in the reign of Henry III. He *m.* Alice, dau. and co-heiress of William de Avenel, of Haddon, co. Derby, and was *s.* by his son,

RICHARD DE VERNON, Lord of Haddon in right of his mother. He *m.* Margaret, dau. of Robert, Baron of Stockport, and acquired by her the manor of Appleby-Parva, and the advowson of Appleby-Magna, in Leicestershire. From this Richard descended the VERNONS of Haddon, Hodnet, Houndshill, Sudbury, and Hilton.

VERDON.—At the General Survey, Bertram de Verdon possessed Farnham, Bucks, and founded the great feudal house of Verdon, whose last male representative, Theobald Lord Verdon, Justice of Ireland, died in 1316.

VAVASOUR —SIR MAUGER LE VAVASOUR, the Norman, is mentioned in Domesday Book, as holding in chief of the Percys, Earls of Northumberland, considerable manors and estates in Stutton, Eselwood, Saxhall, &c. He was *s.* by his son, SIR MAUGER LE VAVASOR, whose son, SIR WILLIAM LE VAVASOR, Lord of Haslewood, was a judge in the reign of HENRY II., and one of the witnesses to the charter of the Abbey of Sawley, in Yorkshire, refounded by Matilda de Percy, Countess of Warwick. To this abbey he himself also made a considerable donation of land. The grandson of this potent knight, SIR JOHN LE VAVASOUR, Lord of Haslewood, *m.* Alice, dau. of Sir Robert Cockfield, and had two sons,

WILLIAM (Sir), his successor, ancestor of the VAVASOURS of HASLEWOOD and SPALDINGTON, co. York.

Malgerus, who had the manors of Denton and Akswith, and was ancestor of the VAVASORS OF WESTON, whose last male descendant, William Vavasor, Esq. of Weston Hall, *d.* 15th Jan. 1133, leaving the children of his sister Ellen, who was *m.* to the Rev. John Carter, his heirs.

WAKE.—The Wakes are mentioned by Brompton as in the immediate train of the CONQUEROR; but it is the opinion of antiquaries that the individual of the name of Wake recorded in the Roll of Battle Abbey, was one of those who being weary of Harold's rule, fled into Normandy, and invited *Duke* WILLIAM; hence the family is supposed to have been of importance prior in the Conquest. From

BALDWIN, LORD WAKE, founder of the Abbey of Brun, who *d.* in 1156, descended, through a long line of eminent ancestors, SIR THOMAS WAKE, a gallant knight, who fought with the Black Prince, and distinguished himself particularly at the battle of Najaru. He was sheriff of Northamptonshire for five successive years in the reign of EDWARD III. By Alice, his wife, dau. and co-heir of Sir John Pateshull, Knt. of Bletso, Bedfordshire, he had a son and heir, SIR THOMAS WAKE, Knt., who *m.* Maud, dau. of Sir Thomas Pigot, Knt., and was *s.* by his son, SIR THOMAS WAKE, Knt., of Blysworth, sheriff of Northamptonshire in 2nd Richard II. He *m.* Margaret, dau. and co-heir of Sir John Philpot, Knt., of Kent, and was *s.* by his son, SIR THOMAS WAKE, Knt., M.P., gentleman of the bed-chamber, and a member of the privy-council to King EDWARD IV. This gentleman was so extensive a landed proprietor in the cos. of Somerset, Northampton, Kent, and the principality of Wales, that he required the designation of "the Great Wake." From Sir Thomas sprang the WAKES of Clevedon, co. Somerset, now represented by Sir CHARLES WAKE, Bt., and WILLIAM WAKE, D.D., Archbishop of Canterbury.

WARREINE.—William de Warren, Earl of Warren, in Normandy, a near relation of the Conqueror's, came into England with that Prince, and having distinguished himself at the battle of Hastings, obtained an immense portion of the public spoliation.

He had large grants of lands in several counties, amongst which were the Barony of Lewes, in Sussex, and the manors of Carletune and Beningtun, in Lincolnshire. So extensive indeed were those grants, that his possessions resembled more the dominions of a sovereign prince, than the estates of a subject. He enjoyed, too, in the highest degree, the confidence of the king, and was appointed joint-justice-general, with Richard de Benefactis, for administering justice throughout the whole realm. When citing some great disturbers of the public peace to appear before him and his colleague, and those refusing to attend, he took up arms, and defeating the rebels in a battle at FAGADUNE, he is said, for the purpose of striking terror, to have cut off the right foot of each of his prisoners. Of those rebels, Ralph Waher or Guader, Earl of Norfolk, and Roger, Earl of Hereford, were the ringleaders. His lordship was likewise highly esteemed by *King* WILLIAM *Rufus*, and created by that monarch, EARL OF SURREY. He m. Gundred, daughter of the CONQUEROR, and had issue two sons and two daughters. This potent noble built the castle of Holt; and founded the priory of Lewes, in Sussex. He resided principally at the castle of Lewes, and had besides Castle-Acre, in Norfolk, and noble castles at Coningsburgh and Sandal. He died in July, 1089: and Dugdale gives the following curious account of his parting hour. "It is reported that this Earl William did violently detain certain lands from the monks of Ely; for which, being often admonished by the abbot, and not making restitution, he died miserably. And, though his death happened very far off the isle of Ely, the same night he died, the abbot lying quietly in his bed, and meditating on heavenly things, heard the soul of this earl, in its carriage away by the devil, cry out loudly, and with a known and distinct voice, *Lord have mercy on me: Lord have mercy on me*. And moreover, that the next day after, the abbot acquainted all the monks in chapter therewith. And likewise, that about four days after, there came a messenger to them from the wife of this earl, with one hundred shillings for the good of his soul, who told them, that he died the very hour that the abbot had heard the outcry. But that neither the abbot, nor any of the monks would receive it; not thinking it safe for them to take the money of a damned person." "If this part of the story," adds Dugdale, "as to the abbot's hearing the noise be no truer than the last, viz.—that his lady sent them one hundred shillings, I shall deem it to be a mere fiction, in regard the lady was certainly dead about three years before." The earl was *s.* by his elder son,

WILLIAM DE WARREN, Earl of Warren and Surrey, who m. Elizabeth, dau. of the great Earl of Vermandois, and widow of Robert, Earl of Mellent, and dying in 1135, left issue, WILLIAM DE WARREN, Earl of Warren and Surrey, a crusader, whose only dau. and heir, Isabel de Warren, m. 1st., William de Blois, Earl of Moreton, natural son of King Stephen, but by him had no issue: and 2ndly, Hameline Plantagenet, (natural brother of Henry II.,) who assumed the surname of Warren, and became Earl of Surrey. By this Earl, Isabel left at her decease, 1198, a son WILLIAM WARREN (*Plantagenet*), Earl of Warren and Surrey, who m. twice, and had with a dau. Isabel, who m. Hugh de Albini, Earl of Arundel, but d. s. p., one son, JOHN WARREN, Earl of Warren and Surrey, who m. Alice, dau. of Hugh le Brun, Earl of March, and half-sister, by the mother, of Henry III., and had one son and two daus., viz.: 1. William, slain in a tournament at Croydon, leaving issue, a son John, Earl of Warren and Surrey, who died s. p. in 1347, and a dau. an eventual heiress, Alice, wife of EDMUND FITZ-ALAN, Earl of Arundel, ancestor, by her, of the Dukes of Norfolk.

WIVELL.—Sir Humphrey d'Wyvill, of the family of Vienville of Normandy, was the Norman thus indicated on the Battle Roll. He acquired a fair share of the spoils of conquest, and seated himself in Yorkshire, where his descendants, the Wyvills of Constable Burton, now represented by MARMADUKE WYVILL, Esq., remain to this day. A Baronetcy exists in the family, but is not assumed.

FINIS.

Clayton and Co., Printers, 16 Hart Street, Covent Garden.

WILLIAM THE CONQUEROR

D'EYNCOURT

ARGENTINE

D'ARCY

ALBINI

BRABAZON

BASKERVILLE

BOURCHIER

BOHUN

BANASTRE

WILLIAM THE CONQUEROR

D'EYNCOURT

ALBINI

BOURCHIER

ARGENTINE

BRABAZON

BOHUN

D'ARCY

BASKERVILLE

BANASTRE

BRUCE

BASTARD

CAMOYS

CHAMBERLAYNE

CORBETT

CHANDOS

COURTENAY

DAUBENEY

DEVEREUX

DISNEY

L'ESTRANGE

FERRERS

GIFFARD

GRANVILLE

HASTINGS

HARCOURT

LOVELL

MAUDE

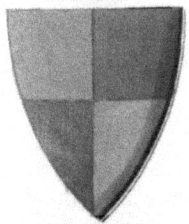
MANDEVILLE

MYNORS

MONTAGU

MONTGOMERIE

NEVILL

POMEROY

PERCY   St LEGER   TIPTOFT

TOUCHET   TRACY   TALBOT

VERE   VERNON   VESEY

VAVASOUR   WARREN   WYVILL

INDEX.

AGUILLON, 14
AINCOURT, 12
ALBEMARLE, 12
ALBINI, 16
ARCHER, 15
ARCY, 15
ARGENTINE, 14
ARUNDEL of Lanhern, Wardour and Trerice, 15
AUDLEY, 13
AVENANT, 15
BANASTRE, 21
BARDOLPH, 17
Bardolph, 14
BARNEWALL, 30
BARRY, 31
BASKERVILLE of Erdisley, Lawton Netherwood, Goodrest, Aberedow, Lambedr, and Clyrow, 18.
BASSETT of Weldon, Drayton, Sapcote, Umberleigh, and Tehidy, 18.
BAUDEWIN, 28.
Beadon of Gotton House, 32.
BEAUCHAMP, 26.
BEAUDEN, 32.
BEAUMONT, 29.
BEKE, 25.
BELLETT, 28.
BELLEW, 32.
BENETT of Laleston, 31.
Benett of Pyt House, 31.
BERNERS, 19.

BERTRAM, 16.
Bertram of Mitford Castle, 16.
BLOUNT, 29.
BLUAT, 24.
BLUETT, 24.
BLUNT, 29.
BODIN, 32.
BOHUN, 20.
BOIS, 22.
BONDEVILLE, 20.
BONETT, 30.
BOTELER, 19.
BOTETOURT, 16
BOTEVILLE, 32.
Botfield, Beriah, Esq., 33.
BOURCHIER, 19.
Boys, John, Esq. of Margate, 22.
BRABAZON, 18.
BRAIBUF, 22.
BRAIOUS, 24.
BRAY, 27.
Bray, Edward, Esq. of Shere, 28.
BRETTE, 30
Brougham and Vaux, Lord, 43.
BROWNE of Beechworth Castle, Walcot, Kiddington, Colstoun, &c., 25.
BRUCE of Clackmannan, Airth, Kennet, Stenhouse, Kilrute, Gartlett, Newton, Kinnaird, &c., 33.
BRYAN, 32.
BURGH, 23.
Burton Robert, Esq. of Longner Hall, 23.

CAMOYS, 34.
CAMVILE, 34.
CAUNCY, 36.
CHAMBERLAINE, 35.
CHAMPERNOWNE, 35.
CHAMPNEY, 36.
CHANDOS, 40.
CHAUNCY, 36.
CHAWORTH, 41.
CHEINE, 36.
CHENEY, 36.
Childe, William Lacon, Esq., of Kinlet, 29.
CHOLMELEY, 36.
CHOLMONDELEY, 36.
Clavering, 56.
CLIFFORD, 37.
Clifford, Lord, the Shepherd, 37.
Clive, E. B., Esq., 15.
Coham of Coham and Dunsland, 46.
COLUMBERS, 36.
COLVILE, 35.
COMYN, 35.
CORBETT, 39.
COURTENAY, 42.
CURZON, 37.
DABERNON, 46.
DABITOT, 48.
DAKENY, 51.
Dakeyne, H. C., Esq., 51.
DAMRY, 46.
DANIEL, 42.
D'ANVERS, 15.
D'ARCY, 15.
D'Arcy, John, Esq. of Hyde Park,
DARELL, 44.
Darell of Calehill, Littlecote, Scotney, &c., 44.
DAUBENEY, 44.
DAUNTREY, 48.
DAWTREY, 48.
DAVENANT, 15.
Davies of Gwysaney, 24.
Davies Owen, Esq., 24.
Dealtry, 49.

De la Warr, 45.
De la Hill, 49.
DE LA BERE, 52.
De la Pole, 44.
De Ros, Lord, 94.
DESPENSER, 43.
DESNY, 46.
DE VAUX, 43.
DEVEREUX, 46.
D'EIVILL, 48.
D'EYNCOURT, 12.
DISNEY of Norton D'Isney and the Hyde, 46.
Drewe of Kilwinny and Meanus, 92.
DRURY, 49.
Drury, George Vandeput, Esq., 49.
Drury of Ickworth, 49.
DUNSTERVILLE, 49.
DYVE or DYNE, 45.
Dymoke, 76.
Dyne, F. Bradley, Esq., 43.
Edwards, Rev. John of the Hayes, 52
ENGAYNE, 52.
Eston, 12.
ESTRANGE, 50.
ESTUTEVILLE, 52.
FAUCONBERG, 54.
FERRERS, 52.
Ferrers of Chartley, Groby, Egginton, and Baddesley Clinton, 53.
FITZ-ALAN, 45.
FITZ-HERBERT, 55.
FITZ-JOHN, 56.
FITZ-WARREN, 56.
FITZ-WILLIAM, 56.
FOLIOT, 53.
Folliott of Ballyshannon, 54.
Folliott, Rev. James, M.A., 54.
FOLVILLE, 55.
Fortibus, William de, 12.
FREVILLE, 54.
FURNEAUX, 56.
Furneaux, James, Esq., 57.
Furneaux, Rev. Tobias, 57.
FURNIVAL, 75.

GAUNT, 60.
GERNON, 58.
GIFFARD, 58.
GORGES, 58.
Gorges, Hamilton, Esq., 58.
Gort, Viscount, 89.
Gournay, 57.
GOWER, 60.
GRANSON, 60.
Granville of Calwich Abbey, 30, 62.
GRENDON, 61.
GRENVILLE, 61.
GRAY, 60.
GREY, 61.
GUINES, 62.
GURDON, 62.
Gurdon of Assington and Letton, 62.
GURNEY, 57.
Gurney of Harpley and West Barsham, 58.
Gurney of Norfolk, 58.
Gurney, Hudson, Esq., F.R.S., 58.
Hackett, Michael, Esq., 66.
HAKET, 66.
HAMOND, 66.
HANSARD, 62.
Hansard, Richard Massey, Esq., 63.
HARCOURT, 65.
Harcourt, George Simon, Esq., 66.
HASTINGS, 63.
Hayman of South Abbey, 67.
HERCY, 65.
Hercy, John, Esq., of Cruchfield, 65.
HERON, 65.
Heyman of Somerfield, 67.
Holford, Anna Maria, 30.
HOVELL, 66.
Howard, Henry, Esq., of Corby, 15.
Hughes of Gwerclas, 24.
HUSEE, 64.
Hussey of Honington, Lyme, Scotney Castle, Westown, &c. &c., 65.
Isaacson, 52.
Jones of Llanarth, 56.
Jones, Thomas Longueville, Esq., 72.

Jones of Lark Hill, 72.
KARRE, 67.
Kerr, 67.
KIRIELL, 67.
Kyrle, John, "Man of Ross," 68.
Kyrle, William Money, Esq., 68.
LACY, 68.
LANE, 72.
Lane, John Newton, Esq., 72.
Langton, Joseph, Esq., 22.
LASCALES, 71.
LASCELLES, 72.
LATIMER, 69.
LEE, 49.
L'ESTRANGE, of Hunstanton, Moystown, &c., 50.
Le Strange, H. L. S., Esq., 34, 50.
Lloyd, Thomas Davies, Esq., 76.
Lloyd, Richard Walmesley, Esq., 53, 100.
LONGUEVILLE, 72.
LOTERELL, 72.
LOVEDAY, 69.
Loveday, John, Esq., of Williamscote, 69
LOVELL, 70.
LOVETOT, 72.
LUCY, 71.
Lucy of Charlecote, 71.
LUTTRELL, 72.
MAINELL, 81.
MAINWARING, 83.
Mainwaring, Capt. R., R.N., of Whitmore, 83.
MALEHERBE, 74.
MALET, 73.
MALTRAVERS, 78.
MANDEVILLE, 74.
Mandeville, Earl of Essex, 12, 74.
Mare, 77.
MARMYON, 76.
MARTEYNE, 76.
Maude of Alverthorpe, 82.
Maude, John, Esq., of Moor House, 82.
MAULE, 81.
MAULEVERER, 82

MAULEY, 77.
Mayer, 77.
Medows, 89.
MELVILLE, 76.
MEYNELL, 82.
MINERS, 82.
MONTAGU, 79.
Montalt, Roger de, 16.
MONTFORD, 80.
MONTGOMERIE, 82.
MONTHERMER, 81.
MONTRAUERS, 78.
Morgan of Arxton, 56.
MORTIMER, 77.
MORTON, 83.
Musgrave, Christopher, Esq., 15.
MYNORS, 82.
Mynors, P. R., Esq., of Treago, 82.
Mytton, 23.
NEVILL, 84.
NOEL, 83.
OLIPHANT, 86.
Packe, Charles James, Esq., 65.
PAINELL, 90.
Parker, R. Townley, Esq., 22.
PECHE, 90.
PERCEVAL, 93.
PERCY, 92.
PERROTT, 90.
Perrott, Sir E. B., Bart., 91.
PEVERELL, 90.
Phelip, Sir William, K.G., 17.
PIERREPOINT, 88.
PIGOTT, 87.
Pleydell, 83.
PLUKENET, 92.
PLUNKET, 92.
POLE, of Radborne, 44.
Pole, E. S. Chandos, Esq., 41, 53.
POMERAY, 91.
Powell, Henry Folliott, Esq., 54.
POWER, 89.
Power, of Curraghmore, Clashmore, Faithlegg, Kilfane, Belleville, &c., 90.
PRENDERGAST, 89.

Prendergast, Major-General Sir J., 89.
Prendergast, T. G., Esq., of Johnstown Park, 89.
Progers, of Werndu, 56.
Pudsey, Florence, 38.
RIDDELL, 94.
Riddell, Sir Walter Buchanan, Bart., 94.
Riddell, Thos., Esq. of Felton Park, 94.
ROCHFORD, 94.
Rochfort of Belvedere, Clogrenane, &c. 94.
Ros, 94.
ROUS, 94.
Rous, T. B., Esq., of Courtyrala, 94.
ST. BARBE, 98.
ST. CLAIR, 95.
ST. GEORGE, 52, 98.
ST. JOHN, 97.
ST. MAUR, 99.
ST. QUINTIN, 96.
ST. LIZ, 97.
ST. LEGER, 95.
St. Leger, of Heyward's Hill, 96.
St. Leger, of Yorkshire, 95.
St. Leger, General, 95.
Sandford, of Sandford, and the Isle of Rossall, 97.
SANFORD, 96.
SEYMOUR, 99.
SINCLAIR, 95.
Skipwith, Sir Gray, Bart., 52.
SOMERVILLE, 96.
Somerville, James S., Esq., of Dinder House, 96.
SOMERY, 97.
Somery, Roger de, 16.
SPENCER, 43.
Stansfeld, 68.
Strangwayes, Mrs. Louisa, 20.
STUTEVILLE, 52.
Talbot, of Bashall, 38, 100.
TALBOT, 100.
Tateshall, of Buckenham, 16.
TIBTOFT, 103
TIRELL, 103.

TOKE, 102.
TOLLEMACHE, 102.
TOOKE, 102.
TOUCHET, 99.
TOUK, 102.
TRACY, 99.
Tracy, Benjamin Wheatley, Esq., Lieut., R.N. 100.
Tracy, James, Esq., 100.
TRUSSELL, 100.
TURBERVILLE, 103.
TURVILLE, 103.
TYRELL, 103.

VAUX, 43.
VAVASOUR, 104.
VERE, 103.
VERNON, 104.
Vernon, of Haddon, Hodnet, Houndshill, Sudbury, and Hilton, 104.
WAKE, 105.
Walker, Joshua, Esq., 30.
Walsham, Sir John, Bart., 25.
WARREN, 105.
West, of Alscot Park, 46.
WYVILL, 106.
ZOUCHE, 95.

www.ingramcontent.com/pod-product-compliance
Lightning Source LLC
Chambersburg PA
CBHW050829160426
43192CB00010B/1956